'Its swashbuckle forces us to re-examine many of our own assumptions and feelings ... As I read these essays I found myself continually wishing to qualify an assertion here, to question an example there. Yet the burden of the case holds. We do need a substantial corrective to the loose, self-indulgent sentiment that corrodes our life and our public policy' Quentin de la Bedoyere, *Catholic Herald*

'Professor O'Hear is brave, and right, to challenge the view that "all you need is love"... empty sentiment is morally destructive' *Daily Telegraph* Leader column

'Most of what Professor O'Hear has to say is sensible and accurate. It amounts to asserting that as a nation we have changed, and for the worse' Alan Watkins, *Spectator*

'The rediscovery of education, the rescue of religion from happy-clappy clerics, the achievement of a just and financially viable welfare system: none of these things will happen if, as a nation, we are unable to face up to the extent to which we have senti-mentalized the world in which we live ... The more people who read this book the better' Chris Woodhead, *Sunday Telegraph*

'We are some years on from 1984 but if these academics are right – and I believe they are – then the world of George Orwell's novel might yet be in the future. A society which loses touch with real-ity is vulnerable to manipulation by those who want only power' Norman Tebbit, *Mail on Sunday*

'*Faking It* scores several direct hits. I found more insight and honesty lurking here than in almost anything else I've read this year' Brendan Walsh, *The Tablet*

FAKING IT

The sentimentalisation
of
modern society

Edited by
DIGBY ANDERSON
& PETER MULLEN

PENGUIN BOOKS

PENGUIN BOOKS

Published by the Penguin Group
Penguin Books Ltd, 27 Wrights Lane, London W8 5TZ, England
Penguin Putnam Inc., 375 Hudson Street, New York, New York 10014, USA
Penguin Books Australia Ltd, Ringwood, Victoria, Australia
Penguin Books Canada Ltd, 10 Alcorn Avenue, Toronto, Ontario, Canada M4V 3B2
Penguin Books (NZ) Ltd, Private Bag 102902, NSMC, Auckland, New Zealand

Penguin Books Ltd, Registered Offices: Harmondsworth, Middlesex, England

First published by St Edmundsbury Press 1998
Published in Penguin Books 1998
1 3 5 7 9 10 8 6 4 2

Set in Monotype Plantin
Printed in England by Clays Ltd, St Ives plc

Contents

The Authors

Dr Digby Anderson is founder Director of the Social Affairs Unit and food columnist for *The Spectator* (London) and *National Review* (New York).

Professor Nicholas Capaldi is currently working in the Department of English at the United States Military Academy, West Point.

Dr Bruce Charlton MD is Lecturer in Psychology at the University of Newcastle-upon-Tyne.

Professor Bruce S Cooper is Professor of Education at Fordham University, New York.

Dr Jo Kwong is a Research Fellow at the Institute of Humane Studies, Fairfax, Virginia.

Revd Peter Mullen is an Anglican clergyman, author and journalist.

Professor Anthony O'Hear is Professor of Philosophy at the University of Bradford and Honorary Director of the Royal Institute of Philosophy.

Dr Dennis O'Keeffe is Senior Lecturer in the Sociology of Education at the University of North London.

Ian Robinson is a former Senior Lecturer in English at the University of Wales in Swansea.

Mark Steyn is media correspondent of *National Review* and of *The* [British] *Spectator*.

Lucy Sullivan is a Research Fellow at the Centre for Independent Studies, Sydney.

Balint Vazsonyi is an internationally-renowned pianist and former Professor of Music at the University of Indiana.

1

The idea of a fake society

introduction and summary

Digby Anderson and Peter Mullen

Engelburt Krull paid unusual attention to the outside of the bottles,...the coiffure. The compressed corks were secured with silver wire and gilt cords fastened with purplish-red wax; there was moreover an impressive round seal — such as one sees on ecclesiastical bulls and old state documents — suspended from a gold cord. The label...bore a number of coats of arms and stars, Loreley Extra Cuvée *all in gold letters and with a female figure arrayed only in bangles and necklaces. Unfortunately, it appears that the quality of the wine was not entirely commensurate with the splendour of the coiffure...The stuff's simply poison.*

Thomas Mann, Confessions of Felix Krull, Confidence Man

Frauds not limited to wine, fake watches and perfumes

Say 'fake' and one thinks of street-sellers touting imitation brand perfumes: the box, the wrapping and the label are all indistinguishable from the genuine French perfume, but the liquid inside is only musty water. In today's society there are fake antiques, fake businesses and investments, and even fake social workers who turn out to be burglars using forged identification to gain entry to a house. Far from helping the householder, they intend to rob him. All these are more or less criminals. Faking is something done by those on the edge of society: villains who set up a stall and are gone by the time the fraud is detected.

But what if faking is not just something on the fringes of society but institutionalised in the respectable operations of society itself? In the last few years, several studies have suggested that the modern vogue for confessional counselling is essentially fake, all show with no proven substance or effect.

Fake schools

It is increasingly clear that the method of teaching known as child-centred education, letting children learn (or not learn) at their own pace, indulging their whims as if indulgence will somehow bolster their self-esteem, learning by play, is a fake. It is not genuine education. It is something worse but dressed up in educational language. This sort of fraud is far more worrying than fake perfume and not only because its effect is more serious — damaging a child's learning and life prospects — but because it is not the exception but the rule and it has spoilt the upbringing of millions of children over a quarter of a century. This is a fake which has been perpetrated not on the street corner but in one of society's principal institutions, recognised by the state and generally accepted as 'the education system'.

What we had in the schools was the *appearance* of education without the underlying reality. Children went to school. Classroom doors opened and closed. Registers were taken. Teachers were employed and paid. But it was a sham. This is the means by which an institution can give all the appearances of existing while actually it is not there at all. And if a fraud can be perpetrated in the education system, where else might there be frauds?

In fact something similar has happened to the social security system. No one doubts that it is still there, for it is bigger and more expensive than ever before. But it does not effectively relieve need and there are signs that it actually encourages dependency. Social security no longer achieves what it was designed to achieve. In reality it produces exactly the opposite, so we can legitimately and aptly call it a fake. Politicians of all parties have noticed the failings of the social security system. They have declared it to be 'inefficient', 'unfair' and 'in need of reform'. But they have missed the point. The social security system is a fake.

A fake church with a fake religion

It is a frightening feeling, akin to the atmosphere in a Kafka novel, when one comes to realise that what was taken for granted, life's familiar and dependable institutions, are not what they seem. This feeling is not confined to state institutions. Everyone knows there has been a huge decline in church attendance in Europe. But there has occurred something far more catastrophic for those who value religion: what goes on in churches these days is not religion. As with modern education and the social security system, the outward forms are still there but the reality, the purpose and the glory of it all have long since departed. There are the pulpits, altars, responses, crosses, the words 'God' and 'prayer'. But in many churches so much has changed, and particularly in the liturgy, that worshippers no longer worship the God they once did. The new emphasis is all on the needs of the gathered community of worshippers, and so the traditional proclamation of an encounter with a transcendent and terrifying God has been played down. What goes on in many churches is still sold as Christianity, but the label is dishonest. If the law applied, today's worship would surely be in breach of the Trades Descriptions Act.

Less formal institutions can be faked too. Neighbours can go through the motions of enquiry after each other long after neighbourliness has left the community. Indeed, the word 'community' seems to be displayed on more and more buildings in bigger and bigger letters once the place has ceased to be a genuine community. The superficial forms of institutions, like ghosts, persist long after the reality has disappeared. Worse, 'community' itself has been debased. It used to mean 'the whole community' or at least 'all the people in this neighbourhood', but now the word means something like its opposite, 'sect'. We hear of 'the black community', 'the gay community' and even once in *The Independent* newspaper, 'the sado-masochistic community'. This perversion of the meaning of 'community' is a sentimental act which results in the fragmentation of the traditional community.

Fakes succeed in a sentimental and superficial society

Fakes work by deceitful appearances. They are a sort of sleight of hand. They succeed only when the 'buyer' is a person who judges merely by the look of the thing. Fakes also offer cheap and easy deals, something for nothing. They are seductive, tempting the buyer with the suggestion that he may instantly realise his dreams. In a similar way we fall for the fake social institutions: we are taken in by them because we are not prepared to make the effort to distinguish between appearance and reality. We fall for the teaching method that shows us happy, playing children and we don't ask searching questions about the school's exam results. Or we pretend that the eradication of poverty can be achieved by easy schemes and without effort by the rich and the poor. As Eliot said, we are forever occupied in a fake existence, 'dreaming of systems so perfect that no one will need to be good'. In religious observances we want the cosy experiences of togetherness and cuddling up to the kindly God, but without any of the old disciplines crucial to traditional faith, Bethlehem without Calvary.

There is a word for the decadent disposition in our culture which falls for the fake: it is 'sentimentality'. The sentimentalist is a person in denial, and what he avoids or denies is reality. He likes to think that good ends can be achieved without unpleasantness. He would rather not be reminded that pain, effort, personal responsibility, self-control and patience are inevitable. He is attracted by schemes which offer good ends without the need for any striving — learning, a just society, community and even pleasure. Most of all the sentimentalist is frightened by the idea that men have a natural capacity for evil. For to admit evil, and the will to evil, is to destroy his world which rests upon the supposition that utopia may be ushered in by the mere adoption of the right plan.

Modern societies face rising crime rates, falling standards in schools, family collapse and widespread confusion about morals and manners. Despite our enormous economic success, something has gone wrong. Two diagnoses are common. One blames bad ideas, theories and policies. The other blames interests and structures and the way society is organised. But really the source of the problem is neither of these. It is something much more basic than organisation, funding or precise policies; more fundamental even than ideologies and philosophies. Sentimentality is a feeling, or rather the distortion of a feeling, deep in the psyche of western civilisation. And this same corruption of feeling is the key to threats to religion and morals, to music and literature, to the relief of pain and suffering by medicine and charity and to the sensible conservation of the earth. A sentimentalist can take over a whole country. Writing about the funeral of Diana, Princess of Wales, Diana, child-like in her self-centredness, Professor Anthony O'Hear finds that funeral the very definition of sentimentality, 'the elevation of feelings, image, spontaneity over reason, reality and restraint'.

Sentimentality's march through the institutions: health, welfare and the environment

This book is about the sentimentalist's progress through the formal and informal institutions of modern life. The authors find the sentimentalist refusing sound judgement in medicine, chasing miracle cures, 'defying' cancers, indulging himself in revelatory counselling. He is there in the medical commentator undermining the necessity for doctors to make judgements. He is a peddler of utopias. The sentimental environmentalist is determined that his utopia shall not be prevented by equivocal or even hostile scientific evidence, or by cost. The sentimentalist bestrides gigantic social engineering projects such as affirmative action — impatient that numerical quotas of income be met and contemptuous of the discrepant natures of those he regards as a homogeneous group.

Sentimentality in music, literature and food

In modern music the sentimentalist indulges himself with no sense of humour. In the modern novel he fakes feelings — and he even fakes having no feelings. At the dinner table he disguises his childish whims as he rejects good food under modish 'isms'. All through, he is a poseur affecting compassion and emotion to the point of self-deception. He conjures illusions in front of the looking-glass. His aim is not understanding, sociability, truth, social betterment or even genuine feeling, though that is its superficial appearance. It is self-image. When sentimentalists have their way with an education policy or a welfare policy, with literature or music, with religion and even with pleasures such as eating and drinking, they drain them of substance, cut them off from reality and leave only a corpse — pleasantly scented but rotting within.

Sentimentality in medicine: nature, health and death cannot be fooled by wishful thinking

Dr Bruce Charlton points to the threat posed by sentimentality to good medical practice. When people are ill, getting old or dying, there are obvious temptations for them, their doctors and their friends to indulge in wishful thinking and reflated forms of sentimentality. If the temptation is given in to, the consequences can be serious for the simple reason that sickness and death are realities of a very prominent sort: they are biological realities. To deny biological facts in medicine is to undermine the practice of medicine. Spectators of disease — viewers watching distant famine victims on television — can be excused their indulgence in a little sentimental sympathy. It may even be natural to exercise this sympathy. But the doctor is not a passive spectator. He is the one who has the power to help or harm.

Here sentimentality is a corruption of good medical practice, since it evades the facts. Patients are tempted to sentimental reactions, one of which may be to deny a diagnosis of, say, cancer. This reaction masquerades as courage. But denial is not the same as courage. Denial turns away from the facts. Courage faces them. 'Plucky resistance and the refusal to despair are all well and good, but wilful self-deception is not.' The result of denial has been a sentimental culture in which it is asserted that every health problem *must* have a cure if only we fight hard enough or spend lavishly enough. Such evasion plays havoc with any attempt to ration scarce money and resources sensibly. Quack doctors and journalists who praise denial as courage thereby incite denial and are engaged in ethically questionable behaviour. Denial of medical facts becomes especially dangerous when it is collective. It creates pressure to join with other relatives or friends in forms of denial which create 'a histrionic world of pretence'.

7

Alternative health frauds: nature is not harmonious

'Green' philosophies of health are another fertile source of sentimental nonsense. For nature is not harmonious: it is a continuous state of trench warfare. The idea that health is natural and sickness unnatural is mistaken. Belief in 'natural' cures arises out of sentimentality. Disease and death are natural. Fringe medicine is a triumph of public relations over scientific and rational evidence. Fringe medicine is a form of wishful thinking. People would like fringe medicine to be true in the way they would like *The Wind in the Willows* to be true: because it's 'nice'. And homeopathy is a fascinating cultural fossil. When there is a serious breakdown in health, people usually abandon their sentimental attachment to fringe medicine and return to orthodox practice — which may at least be able to do something. Fringe medicine diverts resources from where they might really do some good. To introduce fringe treatments into the NHS would result in denying effective treatment to acutely and seriously ill patients in order that the trendy middle classes need not pay for their herbal remedies and acupuncture. Vulnerable sick people and those sentimentally prevented from facing harsh medical truths become the prey of con artists and cranks.

Sentimentality ousts a stoicism necessary where disease is concerned

By contrast, stoicism is a neglected virtue. People used to have an unfussy attitude towards their health, but the media culture has encouraged self-pampering until this has become endemic. This is especially revealed in the phoney occupations of psychotherapy and counselling. Psychotherapists and counsellors are self-selected and in effectiveness worse than amateurs. Therapists are required first to undergo therapy: this is in order that they may be effectively brainwashed into the superstitions and lingo of the cult. But friendship cannot be acquired through a technique. 'Professional help' is a sentimental concept: it is a private shirking of responsibility combined with a public display of cheap compassion. Confessional psychotherapy has no proven effectiveness. What it provides is an excuse for indulgent personal reverie. Moreover, professional counselling undermines the truly caring network of family and friends. Confessional counselling damages both individuals and society.

Sentimentality in medicine undermines the need to make tough decisions. It is the opposite of proper medical practice. It is a cloak for evasive waffle and covert exploitation. Realism in medicine is the antidote to sentimentality.

Sentimentality infects public policy

> *How could the now mammoth...social security system...have ever reached its eminence...if it had been called in the beginning 'political security' or something so mercilessly exact as 'state charity'?*
>
> Robert Nisbet, Fair of Speech

As Dr Charlton identifies sentimentality with the evasion or denial of reality, Professor Nicholas Capaldi suggests that the realities denied are those concerning the baser nature of men. This denial of the tendency to 'sin' is an old one. He begins by demonstrating how modern welfare policy denies the reality of accidents and how it further suggests that all tragedy is eliminable from public life. So when a tragedy occurs, such as a house fire, it is never the fault of the occupant — for 'victims' cannot have faults or sins — but of government social welfare for not providing the 'conditions', that is the funding, in and by which tragic events are not allowed to happen. But actually, the subsistence level of current welfare in 1997 was (even adjusted for inflation) higher than that of middle-class citizens in 1955. It is sentimentality which now decrees that expensive trainers are an essential part of the economic package to which the poor are entitled as by right.

The sentimental denial of the tendency to sin is Pelagian. It denies the felt, psychological reality of Original Sin. It correspondingly insists on the fundamental goodness of human nature. Our modern Enlightenment Project is a new version of Pelagianism as it attempts to define, explain and control the human predicament through science and technology. So the moral agenda which issues from the Enlightenment Project is social engineering and the utopian belief that technological solutions can always be found. Sentimentality insists that the tragedies and unpleasantness of life can be eliminated not by changing ourselves but by changing the environment. In this false understanding, all ills are the fault of 'structures' and 'the system'. The Enlightenment Project substitutes politics for morality and redefines love in terms of social policy.

This leads to the post-Enlightenment paradox: statist social programmes make us free if they remove external constraints; the more powerful the state becomes in removing these restraints the freer we are. As Orwell might have said, some freedoms are more free than others. Modern liberalism takes the Pelagian Enlightenment Project to absurd extremes.

Sentimentality the source of grandiose claims — a creed for people with no patience

Sentimentality ruins good cases. It is insubstantial because it has no roots in reality — in biology, Charlton would say. The desire to make extravagant claims is characteristic of sentimentality, and the tendency to 'gush' is impatient with reality which is complicated and finely balanced. Capaldi demonstrates how the support for 'affirmative action' programmes reveals a rush to put things right. So eager are its proponents to help poor African Americans that they adopt a policy which misses out the stage crucial to their betterment: the self-confidence that flows when they themselves make an effort in their own advancement.

Modern educationalists sentimentalise childhood — the decline of discipline

Truly educated behaviour displays an intelligence modified by genuine feelings. Sentimental education merely substitutes self-absorption for the informed emotions. It is the very softness and easiness of life nowadays which makes this possible. Specifically, the decline of religion has resulted in the growth of nonsensical superstitions such as the innate goodness of children. One might hope that the schools would counteract these superstitions, but state schooling is neither competent nor competitive enough to do so. So it is always susceptible to ideological subversion.

In schools, discipline and obedience have given way to false love and a general slackness. Sentimentalising children frees the teacher from the necessary obligation to deal with their idleness, selfishness and potential for violence: it is so much easier to talk cant about unspoilt young natures in the style of Jean-Jacques Rousseau. The slogan which says that 'middle-class values should not be imposed on children' when it is put into operation also guarantees that the children are deprived of their moral status as human beings. Teachers become sentimentalists when they misunderstand what it is actually to care and provide for the best interests of the child. So they refuse the responsibility of teaching what is right and good, preferring instead the much easier option of 'allowing the child to negotiate the parameters of his own awareness'. What's the difference between that and letting the uninstructed child think and do as he likes?

The new sentimental attitude in teaching can appear to be genuine, loving and caring; but really it is a parody of these virtues and a sort of idolatry. The myth of uninformed self-esteem turns false kindness into a form of cruelty. Not to demand much of pupils means in fact that you are undervaluing them. This aspect of sentimentality is reinforced by another: the denial of fault. For when children should be accorded responsibility and conscience — religion's old 'age of discretion' — they are instead made the objects of determinist understandings of their condition — particularly in that other slogan, 'it is all the fault of society'. This reveals a pernicious combination of sentimentality and pride: for it takes a very arrogant ideologue to claim that poor people have no moral powers.

But there are signs that may spell the end for 'feelgood' as the basis of schooling. Better information about performance has come as a shock to parents and active school markets mean that parents can opt out of bad schools. At the same time, rising standards imposed by governments expose sentimentalism for the vacuousness and cruelty to children that it is. The home personal computer is providing access to knowledge and so ensuring that sentimental schooling is not the only alternative to ignorance.

Sentimental environmentalism's disregard for cost, scientific fact and rationality

Professor Capaldi found sentimentalists in welfare impatient with reality. Professor Bruce Cooper and Dr Dennis O'Keeffe found the same in schools. Dr Jo Kwong finds it in the more extreme sections of the environmentalist movement. Most Britons and Americans support environmentalism in the obvious sense that they would like a more pleasant earth to live on. They are also prepared to pay something of the cost of a sensible conservationism and to adopt reasonable changes in their own behaviour. But this is a world away from the escalating demands and costs of sentimental environmentalism and animal rights.

Just how central sentimentalism can be to the success of a modern institution is shown by the case of environmentalism. Kwong catalogues the extremity of environmentalists' demands and their disregard for the realities of costs and scientific facts. Radical environmentalism has produced some of the most senseless, inane policies and outcomes imaginable. Thirty million dollars is spent in the USA to save habitat for the spotted owl, and six hundred million dollars to avert one death under particular water standards. This sort of environmentalism is not based on rational considerations but on a feelgood, sentimental outlook. For example, on the back of the mantra 'everything is related to everything else', wetlands have achieved divine, untouchable status among American environmentalists.

No rational cost-benefit analysis

Throughout there is the false assumption that the natural habitat is benign and the man-made habitat is harmful. So billions are spent to mitigate the effects of technological products — chlorine in water, ethanol in petrol, solvents in cleaning fluids — effects which are in sum beneficial. Irrational policy is bolstered by the sentimental vision of living in perfect harmony with nature; an expensive delusion based on environmentalism's identification of the earth as a *problem*.

CFCs in aerosols are universally regarded as producers of cancer and destroyers of the ozone layer; but there is no significant and substantial evidence to indicate that CFCs do in fact produce cancer or any increase in ultra-violet radiation. Environmentalists who protest that this world is a filthy place forget how dirty, smelly and disease-ridden was the world of the early twentieth century. Technology has brought an improvement in the quality of life. Why else do we all prefer to buy the most modern products and refuse the obsolescent ones?

The idyllic vision which drives environmentalism is sentimental, expensive and a misuse of resources. What sense does it make to fight for 99 per cent pure water when the world's poor lack access to any water at all? What sense does it make to pursue regulations that devastate local economies and wealth-generation when poverty is the single biggest threat to the environment?

When Christianity is emptied of doctrine, tradition and rules, all that remains is sentimentality

> *There is a species of person called a Modern Christian who draws the full salary of a beneficed clergyman and need not commit himself to any religious belief.*
>
> *Evelyn Waugh*, Decline and Fall

The environmental movement is a new institution. The church is one of the oldest. It is one anchored in history. It has had 2,000 years of practice and experience in exposing humbug, heresy and self-indulgence. Yet here too, we find the atmosphere poisoned by sentimentality. Revd Peter Mullen argues that sentimentality in religion is all that is left when doctrines have been debunked. In particular, the Charismatic Movement has made a new ersatz Christianity out of feelings alone; puerile, manufactured feelings.

Churchy sentimentality tries desperately to be exciting, but the official new prayer book in England, *The Alternative Services Book* is one long-running sentimental euphemism because it disembodies the faith: no vile bodies, no sin, no devil, no worms that devour this body, no death. That makes its repetitive proclamations of redemption and resurrection worthless. Birth and death are alike sentimentalised in the new services. When you see two people hugging and kissing one another in church it is not because they are genuine friends. It is self-indulgent sham. They are being put up to it by the effete atmosphere of touchy-feeliness which surrounds them. The new doctrine is accompanied by a new furniture, especially in the Roman Catholic Church. There are new carpets and armchairs in the sanctuary. 'Contemplative therapy' has replaced the mysterium. Grace is now cheap, forgiveness comes without confession. Judgement, purgatory and hell are hardly mentioned. It is a Pelagian celebration of human niceness.

This extends into all the churches' preoccupation with politics as the public manifestation of politically-correct attitudinising — against arms sales, against tobacco advertising; in favour of a high tax economy for the sake of 'the poor'. It amounts to saying that words do not in fact mean what they say. This is a denial of the Incarnation when the Word was made flesh. Now our too solid flesh is only wordy.

Sentimentality in the novel and poetry
Faking emotion is an effete preoccupation in modern literature. Ian Robinson takes up D H Lawrence's definition of sentimentality as 'working off on yourself feelings you haven't really got'. It is fake emotion as when Victorians writing letters of condolence would scatter water over the page to smudge the ink to simulate tears they had not shed — and grief they did not feel. Nowadays faking feelings with words is general in literature. And sentimentality does its usual work of inhibiting judgement throughout the written word.

We suffer from an extraordinary split, a dissociation of sensibility whereby the release of emotion requires the suspension of the intellect. Robinson identifies three sorts of sentimentality in three different writers. Iris Murdoch, for example, frequently excuses her sentimentality by putting it into the mouth of a character. But still we are left with the awful conviction that she means what her character embarrassingly says — all without the mitigation of irony. *She* it is who really means this sort of thing:

> Her pupils were often dilated so that her eyes became almost black. She had very fine straight hair in a long blob. Her lips were pale and always cold; and when, with my eyes closing, I touched them so childishly with mine, a cold force pierced me like a spear, such as a pilgrim might feel when he knelt and touched some holy, life-renewing stone. Her body was passive to my embraces, but her spirit glowed to me with a cold fire. Her beautiful shoulders... [etc, etc]
>
> Iris Murdoch, *The Sea, The Sea*

Ted Hughes' *Crow* is an example of reverse, obscene sentimentality: it lays claim not to feelings that are too high to be true, but too low. Bad feelings can be phoney too. Martin Amis gets his sales by an affectedly glamorous nastiness which is not true to life. It is all cleverness without judgement. Pretended judgement. Sentimental judgement. Sentimentality is inappropriate emotion. Robinson speculates that should ever sales of Amis's novels collapse, he would be able to make a living reporting football and darts, and there would be no way of knowing whether he was doing it tongue-in-cheek or not. In a sentimental literary world, satire becomes impossible. Serious writing requires irony, but sentimentality is un-ironic. It is cleverness without judgement.

Classical composers used to blow away sentimentality with humour: not any more

The great antidote to posturing of all kinds is a sense of humour. Balint Vazsonyi, in describing decadent trends in music, claims that a blast of wit is what is needed to blow sentimentality away. Throughout the eighteenth century, humour in music was a preventative against the tendency to sentimentalise. But nineteenth-century composers emphasised the place of the self in musical creation and the result was a burgeoning sentimentality. And the sentimental preoccupation with self destroys compositional art. Pity is devilish because it ruins all the best tunes. The dissolution of music preceded the dissolution of morality, vocabulary and politics. The fad for 'period' instruments and performances is highly sentimental and incongruous: if 'period' instruments had been superior, they would not have been replaced by improvements. It is a mark of the sentimentality of 'period' performers that you cannot joke with them.

Sentimentality and puritanism are the enemies of civilised eating

Puritanism is traditionally considered the opposite and the enemy of refined, enjoyable eating and drinking. But an even worse enemy, argues Dr Digby Anderson, is the food sentimentalist. He may be a 40-year-old who is still a baby at table, squeamishly refusing smells, tastes and textures because of whims which he should have outgrown. He may be purely self-indulgent, a grown-up human who eats like a pig, or the food-grazer who mistakes fancy for appetite, so the two slices of bread encasing the microwaved sausage and dribbling ketchup is abandoned moments after it is demanded. Solitary consumption of instant foods is unimaginative and antisocial. In cooking, indulgence without discipline makes for poor fare.

There are more refined types of food sentimentalist than the whimsical pig. His girlfriend, for example, is puritanical and high-minded and will eat only 'natural' foods — not comprehending that most of her approved dietary intake is produced according to exactly the same processes which she would despise as 'instant', 'synthetic' and 'unnatural'. Food cranks are environmental sentimentalists. Food sentimentality is wasteful of resources.

The health sentimentalist does not see food as a source of pleasure or even as a fuel, but as threats to her longevity, intimations of obesity and a conspiracy by food companies to murder her with a heart attack. Good cooking and good eating are neither sentimental nor puritanical: they require a knowledge of tradition, the cultivation of regular habits in stocking the larder and using the kitchen; above all hospitality, etiquette and restraint.

Where does this sentimentality come from? The point at which sentimentality corrupted Western tradition

Sentimentality is a relatively new phenomenon. We don't find much of it in Plato. Lucy Sullivan describes the mixing of its elements in three ages, the Enlightenment, the Romantic Age and the Modern World.

The Enlightenment transformed Christianity. It replaced individual guilt and repentance with a political vision in which the problems of the world were due to conditions. These were to be remedied by a political programme and by progress and knowledge. The denial of guilt opened the way for a Romantic view of human passion as naturally good.

Romanticism glorified unrestrained passion. Though the Victorians added restraint and caution to the expression of the feelings, this restraint was not in accordance with the principles of external doctrine or dogma — because the nineteenth century had already witnessed the demise of religious authority. And it degenerated into a merely creepy niceness, a oleaginous fastidiousness, to use a word common at the time, a *vapour*. Nineteenth-century sentimentality tried to connect the emotional luxuries of Romanticism with Christianity. But the burgeoning sentimental attitude produced a dissociation between feelings and morality, for it employed emotion in the Romantic mode of self-pleasuring rather than in accordance with Christianity's binding emotion of moral action. So Romanticism furthered the sentimentalising of the feelings.

Sentimentality given a revolutionary gloss
In our own age, and with the failure of Communism, it is romantic sentimentality which has successfully sold egalitarianism. This Romantic sentimentality can be seen in the 'Green' movement and it was there in the 1960s slogans 'flower power' and 'make love not war'. It chiefly manifested itself in the spectacle of gilded youth acting up against the exceptionally benign paternalism of the welfare state, made possible by massive financial support from a technological culture despised by those doing the acting up.

The Romantic sentimentality, which 200 years ago idealised rural life, has now been transferred to the working class, to 'the oppressed'. This loss of confidence in the values and competence of middle-class virtues has led in less than 20 years to a dependent underclass: the drug-addicted, the violent, the unemployed, and the promiscuous. And the 'lifestyle' of this underclass is sentimentalised (as poverty once was) as 'real life'. The word 'disadvantaged' is used to identify the underclass with the stultifying badge of dependency. In the twentieth century, Romantic insouciance is supported by the welfare state.

Sentimentality thus disempowers and demoralises the poor. This has now reached the extreme limit in which we even sentimentalise crime and so abolish the moral distinction between right and wrong.

Social justice is made unjust because its proponents will not relate input to output — responsibility and integrity to social conditions. No one is to blame for anything — except wicked conservatives and capitalists. And the new brand of sentimental saints — their actual amounts of wealth and privilege, which are often considerable, notwithstanding — are those who 'identify' with the underclass. Sentimentality tries to transpose into the public sphere moral imperatives which can operate only in the private sphere and to replace personal forgiveness and love by a political welfare system.

The many faces of sentimentality — all ugly and dangerous

There are surely many other important areas of modern life which need to be analysed in terms of their sentimentality. There is a certain sort of feminism which is so keen to advance women's equal rights with men that it refuses to recognise obvious basic biological differences between the sexes. The physical work involved in fire-fighting and the military, for example, makes demands which the sexes cannot equally fulfil. The consequence of yielding to unrealistic demands for equality has actually been to downgrade standards of training and expertise in those tasks so that women can meet them. 'Rights' talk generally shows this impatience with reality. It is most clearly revealed in the cant political term that this or that inequality, suffering or hazard is 'unacceptable'. But sensible societies know there will always be some suffering, hazard and inequality. They try to reduce them, but it is pure sentimentality to pout like a child and 'find it totally unacceptable' that even one person should live in conditions like this or be exposed to this risk or have less of whatever than another person.

The growth of gesture — sentimental politics

Most of the politicians who say such things know they cannot change matters so as to meet their ludicrous standards of acceptability. It is done for show, to strike a pose, and not for the benefit of anyone. Indeed, it may actually harm those who suffer. They need a realistic policy. But the fact, acknowledged by commentators of very different political persuasions, that modern government is increasingly not about effectual policies but about gestures, shows how sentimentality is the key to understanding modern politics. Gesture politics are chosen not for effect but affect. Politicians attempt to be 'seen' to be 'taking' this or that problem 'seriously' — but serious is the last thing they are. Their interest is in how they will he received or seen and, of course,

17

whether they will be popular in some immediate sense. They fulfil several characteristics of sentimentality in their denial of reality, their concern with appearance and their self-indulgence.

If the whole of government is susceptible to sentimentality in all the areas it affects such as social security, foreign affairs, devolution policy and overseas aid policy, there is still one institution which outdoes government in the sentimentality stakes: the media. Mark Steyn shows the systematic replacement of thought by feelings in the modern media. Facts are ignored in favour of versions which arouse extreme emotions. The news is turned into soap opera. There is little interest in principle and less in real characters — stereotypes strut the stage. Public affairs becomes entertainment.

This short review has shown just how deep and broad is the permeation of sentimentality in modern society. But it has also fleshed out a picture of the different faces of sentimentality. There is the baby, stamping its feet in impatience with the realities of the world, pouting when its desires are not immediately fulfilled, wriggling against the restraints of reason and discipline. There is the self-righteous carer, the smirking manipulator of images, the salesman of easy options. All of them traffic in fakes and frauds which are socially costly. Fakes, of course, rarely last for ever. But the sentimental appetite of modern society ensures there will be new ones to replace those which are discredited. It is not the fake which society must confront, but its own voracious sentimental appetite. Does 'voracious' seem an exaggeration? Is sentimentality really as widespread and central to modern society?

There is a better answer to these questions than an argument — an event. The funeral of Diana, Princess of Wales, was sentimentality personified and canonised. In that mob grief, feeling, image and spontaneity were elevated above reason, reality, and restraint and the full extent of modern sentimentality made available for anyone with eyes to see.

2

Life before health

against the sentimentalising of medicine

Bruce Charlton

Talking of our feeling for the distress of others; — Johnson: 'Why, Sir, there is much noise made about it, but it is greatly exaggerated.' Boswell: 'But suppose, Sir, that one of your intimate friends were apprehended for an offence for which he might be hung.' Johnson: 'I should do what I could to bail him and give any other assistance; but if he were once fairly hanged, I should not suffer…Sir that sympathetic *feeling goes a very little way in depressing the mind.'*

James Boswell, The Life of Samuel Johnson

Denying unpleasant realities while proclaiming one's concern

Sentimentality comprises two major elements, private avoidance and public sensitivity. On the one hand, there is a shrinking from the need to deal with unpleasantness by denying it, on the other hand a social advertisement of concern, pity and generous spirit. At best sentimentality is an understandable weakness of nerve in response to sheer terror; at worst it is a form of image-management, a mask for manipulation.

Sentimentality constitutes an important problem when it occurs in the arena of health and medicine. Pain, sickness, ageing, disease and death — these are perhaps the least appropriate circumstances for indulging in evasion. There is no legitimate place for public posturing when dealing with suffering humanity. Yet confrontation with the intractable realities of human sickness and frailty can be a powerful inducement to retreat into wishful thinking, or to engage in promoting oneself as an individual of exceptional compassion.

In what follows I will suggest the roots of medical sentimentality and describe some of its commoner and more damaging forms. Sentimentality in medicine is usually based upon a false understanding of biological actuality and the human condition. Sentimentality ought to be resisted as an attitude damaging to the proper practice of medicine.

The media culture inspires pseudo-responses

When, as so often in contemporary life, people find themselves in the role of passive spectator in a frightening media spectacle, then striking a sentimental pose may be the most natural response.[1] Not to respond in such a fashion would be considered freakish. To fail to express sympathy for the victims of a disaster, or condemnation for the perpetrator of an atrocity, or to abstain from taking up a viewpoint on the sexual desirability of an actor or actress in the news, is taken as evidence of some peculiar moral deficit.

Such discourse is, of course, utterly without effect on the events under consideration. Yet the having and voicing of opinion is taken with great seriousness. All this could be seen as an attempt on the part of members of the public to play the role of a 'caring' bystander in a virtual world of mega-scale heroes and villains, beauties and beasts. In this false but epic realm the public are in the position of consumers who goggle and pay, laugh and cry, but provide no help and take no action. The social players in contemporary life are often remote or unreal. This is an encouragement to indulge in sentimentality untrammelled by social consequences. The upshot is a habit of generating pseudo-responses to bogus situations, and this is hard to break when it comes to health matters.

Yet in medicine, when circumstances are grave and demand to be dealt with and we have the power to help or harm, then sentimentality is an indulgence. Then we are dealing with nature, and nature will not be fooled. In the end sentimentality will fail and we must yield to stark actuality — the less prepared for having avoided thinking about it or acting to ameliorate its consequences.

The sentimental refusal to accept bad news

One form commonly taken by medical sentimentality relates to bad news.[2] The patient may refuse to accept a poor medical prognosis, or the doctor may conceal such a prognosis. Of course, prediction is always imprecise and medical prognostication is often a fallible science. Yet reasonable doubt is not the same as a systematic refusal to confront that which is unwelcome.

Denial is importantly different from courage. Denial is a turning away from that which is feared, while courage is a confrontation with fear and overcoming of its inhibitions. The distinction seems clear, but 'human interest' stories on medical topics routinely confuse the two. No celebrity 'has' cancer, instead they are described as 'fighting' cancer. Indeed, there is a whole school of subjectivist thinking about ageing, disease, death and the other unavoidable biological realities, that downplays the inevitable and the intractable, and instead asserts that for every health problem there 'must' be an answer — somewhere, somehow, if only you fight hard enough, shout loud enough, travel far enough — and shell out enough money.

There is a genre of medical morality tale that takes this *quest* form: whether as a novel, film, play or 'docu-drama'. For instance, the hero is informed that he suffers from a disease known to be incurable or fatal (although we are seldom told the degree of certainty of the prognosis). Instead of preparing for the likely consequences, he angrily denounces the doctors — asserting that he will 'prove them wrong' — and embarks on a quest for the holy grail of a cure. After a suitable period of downs and ups, a solution is found — usually from a surprising direction. The 'experts' are confounded and humbled to general acclaim.

This familiar narrative is the veiled expression of a comprehensive failure to come to terms with biology. Such behaviour is perhaps understandable as a blotting out of fear. The behaviour of those doctors, quacks and journalists who encourage patients in their deluded questing is equally comprehensible in terms of financial interest and self-seeking. But although understandable, such behaviours can hardly be seen as admirable. This species of sentimentality holds up evasion as an example of fortitude.

Sentimentality maintains 'positive thinking' in the face of unpleasant medical facts

Plucky resistance and the refusal to despair are all well and good, but wilful self-deception is not. This common phenomenon is what William James described as the 'religion of healthy-mindedness'.[3] It occurs where a belief in 'the power of positive thinking' is employed to eliminate from consideration even the possibility of negative consequences .

In the case of medicine, positive thinking is supposed to be therapeutically beneficial in its own right — by means of pseudo-scientific psychosomatic rationale. The idea that state of mind can influence the body is pumped-up from an occasional observation to a fundamental therapeutic principle. Medical healthy-mindedness therefore involves an assertion that matter can be *mastered* by mind; that subjective psychology has command over objective biology; that proper attitudes will inevitably lead on to improved outcomes. In effect, prognosis is enhanced by its denial. For example, 'visualising' (ie imagining) a cancer and its defeat by the body's immunological defences, is supposed to effect a cure. Wherever there is a grave or intractable medical prognosis, there will be found the prophets of healthy-mindedness advocating all manner of positive thinking: spiritual renewal, religious transformation, stress-reduction, psychotherapy, meditation, yoga, encounter groups; and other ways of inducing the requisite harmonious attitude such as massage and 'natural' (ie restrictive) diets.

A state of dogmatic optimism in the face of the outright failure of positive thinking to achieve its aims is surprisingly easy to maintain — so long as there is rigidly-enforced collusion from others. Friends, family and physicians (as well as other types of therapists) may be enlisted to the task on the basis of helping 'maintain a brave face'. Indeed, they may themselves have inculcated and encouraged the optimistic delusions for reasons of their own.

It is often assumed that this kind of thinking will 'at least, do no harm'. Yet once a regime of compulsory sentimentality is established, the patient enters a histrionic world of pretence, and it becomes an absolute imperative that nobody be allowed to shatter the brittle crust of fantasy. This profoundly undignified state is maintained by the fear that if reality should break in, it will cause a catastrophic reaction, collapse of morale and death.

This is the sinister side of the religion of healthy-mindedness: pessimism is the ultimate sin, and bad outcomes are the just deserts of those who fail to be healthy-minded. It is one of the most poignant tragedies that a kindly-intended desire to avoid distress can lead down a slippery slope of deception and blame until the end of a life may become trivialised by an atmosphere of hysterical denial.

Belief in 'natural' cures arises out of sentimentality

'Green' philosophies of health are another fertile source of sentimental nonsense. Green health beliefs are based upon several linked notions. One is a myth of the essential 'harmony' and 'balance' of uncorrupted nature. Another concerns the beneficent effects of the 'natural' in contradistinction to the harmful influences of the human. There is a hostility to the technological, modern and secular; and a prejudice in favour of the simple, ancient and 'spiritual'. A further tendency is the paranoiac practice of tracing the ills of contemporary life to a conspiracy of industry, 'big business', multinational companies, right-wing governments and 'international capitalism' in general.

A belief in the 'balance of nature' is very common — and not just in the Green movement.[4] This sees the biological world as a harmonious equilibrium characterised by negative-feedback, so that disruptive change in one aspect is neutralised by compensatory change in another aspect, and so the balance is restored. This view of the world as a homeostatic system has been reinforced by the idea of Gaia, whereby the planet earth is seen as regulating its own state of biophysical harmony — either intentionally as a quasi-goddess, or as a fortuitous consequence of evolutionary and chemical factors.

The 'balance of nature' is one of the most persistent of biological misunderstandings. Any apparent 'equilibrium' in the natural world is not harmonious in its essence, being more like a stalemate in the continuous trench warfare of adversaries than a concord of co-operators. In biology, conflict and competition is the rule and default state.[5] Genuine harmony and co-operation do, of course, frequently occur in nature; but such co-operation invites specific explanation in each instance — it is not a spontaneous tendency that can be assumed as a given.[6] Green policies generally seek to restore an assumed 'natural' balance within the human organism and among living things (frequently this balance encompasses both the physical and spiritual worlds). A spontaneous tendency for harmony is taken for granted, and the task for Green activists is simply to *allow* this tendency to become manifest by diminishing the influence of humans in general and 'big business' in particular.

If this should be achieved then health problems will (it is presumed) largely disappear without the need for interventionist medicine, pharmaceuticals or technology. In other words, health is natural, while sickness is seen as a consequence of human intervention upsetting the balance of nature. This alluring perspective is built upon the common observation that — left alone — things will often put themselves right. When tired we sleep, when hungry we eat, and disease is frequently self-limiting. And in the past, the best medical strategy was usually 'therapeutic nihilism' — in other words, the doctor should diagnose, explain, arrange for 'tender loving care' and let events take their course — because the available treatments did more harm than good. For minor and intractable conditions this is still the best clinical strategy.

But this tendency for self-healing is not a case of spontaneous harmony. It is 'natural' only in the sense that it is a consequence of natural selection which has (over many thousands of generations of our ancestors) equipped humans with the means to resist infection, heal wounds, fight disease, etc.[7] But it is equally 'natural' for us to have random accidents, for our bodies to be successfully invaded by more rapidly evolving creatures such as bacteria and viruses, for the various ageing processes to cause a decline in function, and for our defence mechanisms to break down and fail from time to time, or even turn against us in 'auto-immune' diseases.

Death and disease — pain and suffering of the most extreme sort — are as 'natural' a part of the world as harmonious co-operation: and considerably more common, as gardeners, pet owners and watchers of wildlife documentaries ought to be aware. The purpose of medicine — its special role — is often exactly to *prevent* what is 'natural' from running its course, and instead to impose a state of affairs that is more gratifying to human aspirations.

Fringe medicine: a form of wishful thinking

Fringe medicine is another major focus of sentimentality, and one bound up philosophically and in practice with the Green perspective on health. Fringe medicine is also called 'alternative' and 'complementary' medicine. These nomenclatures seem to beg important questions and 'fringe' is preferred here as being less prejudiced.

Fringe remedies are found in every chemist and 'health food' shop; books on the subject abound, and a very high proportion of the population have at some time tried out one or another of the various schools. A successful propaganda campaign has won over considerable public opinion to the idea that fringe remedies have a useful place alongside modern medicine. A surprising number of orthodox medical practitioners are also under the impression that evidence has accumulated to demonstrate that the claims of some fringe therapies (such as acupuncture and homeopathy) have been vindicated. Osteopathy and chiropractic are at least semi-respectable, despite their ludicrously irrational theoretical underpinnings; and many people have dabbled in aromatherapy, flower remedies, healing crystals and other consumer artefacts which may be purchased relatively cheaply on the high street.

Yet there is absolutely no reason to believe that any of the fringe medical systems have any specific and beneficial therapeutic effects.[8] A few well-publicised research studies have been canvassed as having demonstrated 'statistically significant' effectiveness — for instance in homeopathy — but these studies are either flawed, or else the results are subject to alternative and more likely explanations. Furthermore, fringe therapies always report their 'successes' in exactly those chronic, unpredictable, relapsing and remitting conditions for which benefits are so hard to demonstrate; conditions such as asthma, excema, hay fever, multiple sclerosis, rheumatoid arthritis, headache and back pain.[9]

Publication bias favouring positive results, sloppy methods and poor control group matching explain the apparent instances of effective fringe medicine. And fringe treatments have never been found to be useful in conditions with a predictable and uniformly bad prognosis — they do not cure lung cancer, or diabetes, nor can they re-implant a severed finger, nor cause the stump to regrow. In this respect, nothing has changed over the past couple of decades: there have been no breakthroughs in fringe medicine. Its new-found respectability is a triumph of public relations over scientific and rational evidence.

It is hard to say how seriously fringe medicine is taken. The extraordinary metaphysical systems that serve to rationalise it, mostly conjured up from half-understood scraps of ancient (or pseudo-ancient) history and mythology, do not themselves appear to command much belief. Even professional fringe practitioners themselves tend to pick-and-mix among a range of mutually incompatible explanations and therapies on the basis of ill-defined instinct and aesthetic preference (although such eclecticism may be due to lack of intellectual rigour rather than a sophisticated, integrative understanding of alternative pathology).

On the whole, fringe remedies appear to be used alongside conventional medicine, rather than as a replacement for it: they are additional rather than 'alternative' to conventional health services. However, the amount of money spent on fringe therapies signifies that they are fulfilling some role in our culture.

People would *like* fringe medicine to be true, just as they would like *The Wind in the Willows* to be true. Fringe medicine is simpler, nicer, (usually) safer, more wholesome and more spiritually resonant than real, orthodox medicine. Homeopathy, for instance, is an aesthetically appealing system. Elegant, arcane: it is — we feel — exactly how medicine ought to be. This derives from its roots in the world of the eighteenth-century gentleman-physician: homeopathy is a fascinating cultural fossil.[10] Unfortunately, the principles from which the homeopathic system has been logically derived are themselves based upon nothing more than unsupported assertion and hopeful analogy; and the toxicity data which underpins homeopathic remedies was gathered using laughably naive methods. And homeopathy is by far the most coherent and intellectually rigorous of the fringe systems —

there is even less reason to believe in the others.

Furthermore, fringe practitioners are considerably cheaper than orthodox ones, which allows longer private consultations. Their symptom-based systems mean that unorthodox practitioners often make better use of the placebo effect. If only it worked, it would all be marvellous! But commonsensical people know deep down that fringe systems of practice are all metaphysics and mystique — hokum and hogwash. When anything serious happens they will turn from these lifestyle games and resort to real medicine; which may be nasty, unspiritual and dangerous, but at least offers the potential to be effective.

Fringe medicine diverts resources from where they might really do some good

Among commonsensical people, the main harm of fringe medicine is to waste money and to encourage a sentimentally credulous and dependent attitude which spills over into the rest of life. At worst, this has led some people to propose introducing fringe medicine into the British National Health Service, on the basis that medical treatments (even when useless) ought to be universally available regardless of ability to pay. In practice, and given the fixed health budget, this would result in denying effective treatment to acutely and seriously ill patients in order that the trendy middle classes need not pay for their herbal remedies and acupuncture.

However, among the seriously or terminally ill who seek help from fringe therapies the harm may be more profound.[11] These harms include the failure to diagnose and obtain effective treatment for real disease. Another problem is the pseudo-diagnosis of non-disease — fringe practitioners often make diagnoses of non-existent diseases which only they can detect or cure (eg, the various forms of phoney 'allergy' in Clinical Ecology, or the fake 'endocrine' disorders diagnosed from the soles of feet by reflexologists). This labelling can create much misery and distress, and itself induce a subjective state of illness. By such means, vulnerable sick people become the prey of con artists.

Another source of harm from fringe medicine is loss of life spent in the vain pursuit of that which is unattainable. Instead of using one's life to pursue personal goals, enjoying the pleasures of each day and eventually coming to terms with death, irreplaceable time is spent in a whirlwind of futile and self-directed activity, pursuing the chimera of cure from one school of fringe medicine to another.

Futile chasing after the unattainable is a predictable consequence of surrendering oneself to the sentimental credulity required as a prerequisite to seeking help from fringe therapists. There are dozens of panaceas on offer, the practitioners will seldom turn away a client or fail to diagnose a potentially 'treatable' ailment, and scientifically-speaking there is nothing to choose between them. Having tried homeopathy without success, why not have a shot at acupuncture, chiropractic, iridology, Bach's flower remedies? And so on down the slippery slope.

Stoicism: a neglected virtue

Stoicism can be defined as an undemonstrative acceptance of adverse events. Although seeking a resolution to one's problems is sensible if there is an answer to be had, nevertheless when all reasonable avenues are exhausted stoicism has a vital role to play. Perhaps few can aspire to stoical endurance *in extremis*, yet it used to be common for people to have an attitude to health that was pragmatic and unfussy. They simply wanted to 'get on with life' and pursue their own business so long as they were free of illness.

It would be foolish to discount the many potential benefits that modern medical practice has to offer. For example, there have been massive reductions in premature deaths from infectious diseases such as tuberculosis, cholera, diphtheria and smallpox. This must count as real progress. Curative and reparative treatments have also substantially added to the expectation of life.[12] And the quality of life has been enhanced by improved methods for alleviating pain, the development of anaesthetics, the correction of deformity and disfigurement, and restorative surgery. These too have surely increased the sum of human happiness. To fail to take advantage of these possibilities would be to seek martyrdom, not to practice stoicism.

However, there is an exaggerated belief in the capability of medicine to guarantee good health and long life. Many areas of disease remain largely untouched by medical advances. As more humans begin to approach the biological limits of lifespan and experience the progressively declining functions typical of senescence, we might anticipate that suffering for many years from an accumulation of chronic, degenerative and dementing diseases will become more prevalent.[13] Once the available remedies have been applied to alleviate symptoms, much that is intractable will remain. Stoical endurance and perseverance in the face of difficulty will then become an attribute greatly to be prized.

When all is said and done, the fundamental biological realities of disease, ageing and death remain to be confronted. That much is unchanged. Lives that are not terminated prematurely and abruptly will often end in this fashion. Effective cures and remedies are few and far between, discovered only by labour-intensive and costly means, and imperfect in their activity. When disease is pushed back on one frontier it will re-emerge to attack from new and unexpected directions. The problems of life might be delayed and diverted; they cannot be eluded.

Psychotherapy and counselling: sentimental professions

Perhaps the most egregious example of sentimentality in contemporary Western society, and the one which most powerfully undermines stoicism, is the area of psychotherapy, counselling, psychoanalysis and the other confessional 'talking cures'. The combination of therapeutic ineffectuality, spiritual arrogance and moral bankruptcy mark out psychotherapy as one of the great scandals of our era.[14]

Precisely defining psychotherapy is difficult since there are at least 400 schools current. But the common factor that unites these schools, and sets them apart from the effective psychological techniques of behaviour therapy and cognitive therapy, is a belief in the intrinsic virtue of *confession*.[15] The crux of psychotherapy and counselling is a conversation in which the client unburdens himself frankly and fully.

Such relationships bring with them a Freudian baggage — the notion that it is therapeutically and personally beneficial to 'talk through' feelings, experiences, opinions; and especially to bring to light memories of secret or shameful events (usually from childhood) of a kind that are supposed to be the cause of current problems. This type of one-sided confessional relationship is a vital component of many 'brainwashing' techniques. It creates an emotional reliance upon the confessor; the more secret and shameful the things confessed the greater is the desire for that 'absolution' only the confessor can give.

Freud called this state of deliberately induced dependence the 'transference reaction', and claimed it could be interpreted as the re-emergence of unresolved childhood conflicts with the parent. He also placed it at the centre of the therapeutic psychoanalytic relationship, where it has remained. This was a shrewd move for the would-be psychoanalytic profession, because although there was no shred of evidence for the therapeutic benefits of transference, inducing transference by means of confession provides the perfect excuse for creating long-term dependence of a client upon his therapist — thus guaranteeing the therapist's livelihood.

Confessional psychotherapy provides an excuse for indulgent personal reverie

The question of therapeutic effectiveness may briefly and unambiguously be dealt with: confessional psychotherapy has *no specific therapeutic effectiveness*.[16] When tested under controlled conditions there is no difference in therapeutic outcome between trained and untrained personnel, no difference according to length of training, no difference between schools of practice... In other words, the therapeutic benefits of counselling are the result of a placebo effect, and are non-specifically due to supportive conversation. Expertise in psychotherapy cannot be inculcated, and the techniques and theories (Freudian, Jungian, Adlerian, Kleinian, Rogerian, etc, etc) are irrelevant to effectiveness. The conclusion is that professional therapists are no better at the job than Joe Bloggs.

Indeed, there is good reason to believe that professional counsellors are usually *worse* than Joe Bloggs. Psychotherapists are largely self-selected, but unfortunately the self-selection leads to recruitment of a considerable number of individuals whose motivations are suspect. It is an open secret that psychotherapy differentially attracts practitioners from among those who have themselves suffered emotional and psychological problems and are (consciously or implicitly) seeking help for their own difficulties through the psychotherapeutic relationship.

Of course, having suffered from emotional or psychological difficulties oneself does not *necessarily* mean that one is inappropriately motivated or unable to help others. On the other hand, having a past or present history of psychiatric troubles is certainly not a *recommendation* for dealing with people who are, by definition, vulnerable. It makes little sense for recruitment to be based upon an incapacity rather than ability.

The various schools of psychotherapy are best considered, not as therapies — which they are not — but as a collection of quasi-religious *cults*. These employ professional brainwashing techniques in order to win converts to the cause. Because although counselling techniques do not have specific therapeutic benefits, they do often induce distinctive personality changes, in particular dependence on the therapist and a new way of interpreting human affairs.

Such outcomes do not constitute an improvement in personal functioning, so much as an *initiation* into the role of acolyte. This also explains why therapists must themselves undergo therapy. They too need brainwashing to work within the cult. In real medicine it is not considered necessary to undergo a treatment in order to practice it properly.

As with any cult, the convert claims vast benefits and positive transformation while the convert's previous friends and family can see only wilful blindness and fanaticism. And there is no arguing with converts — they have had internalised a set of standards of evidence and special methods of reasoning that render ineffective normal rational arguments. Indeed, to argue against psychotherapy is itself a sign of sickness; a pathological denial of revealed truth.

Counselling damages individuals and society

In the end, the rise of counselling can be seen as a triumph of hope over common sense. Everyone hopes for true friendship with someone who is kind, understanding, wise, a good listener... But common sense informs us that it is an absurdity to imagine that true friendship can be had for the asking — paid for on an hourly basis — or that its benefits can be encapsulated in a technique, trained, and deployed impartially.

We have no reason to believe that the fundamental problems of life — birth, love, loss, happiness, sadness, death — are amenable to solution by applying a special technique of managing conversations. Nor is it plausible to imagine that the negative, etiolated world view embodied in psychotherapy makes a satisfactory religious basis for a conversion experience. The counselling cult is a confidence trick that preys upon wishful thinking — the craving that perennial questions can be answered and intractable miseries dissolved by 'talking through' things with a hired expert. The problem is genuine, it is the response that is phoney. We seek edifying conversation, we seek to explore with another person our own place in the world, clarify our own natures and goals, and come to terms with the events that occur in our lives. The best that can be managed is for each of us to seek out persons of known good will and good sense to speak with; and we will do the same for them — in other words, we seek a *true* friend. And for such purposes psychotherapists and counsellors are not the best; nor even second or third best. If there is no true friend existing or available, and no trusted family member, and no professional already known to be of solid and sympathetic character (eg doctor, priest, lawyer, teacher) — *then*, and only then, may a paid conversationalist be a suitable last resort.

Yet it is routinely implied that counselling is not merely a poor fourth, but the very best assistance that can be given to desperate and damaged people. The cant phrase, 'you need professional help', says it all. It says that when someone is deeply troubled, they 'need', and perhaps 'deserve', help from the self-styled experts in life itself. This is not an expression of serious concern; it is sentimentality: a private shirking of responsibility combined with a public display of cheap compassion.

Counselling is a cultural strategy that is profoundly damaging for both individuals and society at large. In effect, close family, trusted friends and familiar professionals are being 'warned off' conversing with their loved ones, when the loved ones are deeply troubled or when the issues are grave. This is because friends and family lack 'training' in the recommended techniques. What is being suggested here is that people who care about us (genuinely *care* that is; as opposed to being members of a 'caring profession') are disqualified from being helpful because they are too 'involved', too 'judgmental', too 'directive' and because they have not mastered the theory and skills of one or another of the schools of psychotherapy.

If such a counselling culture becomes established and entrenched, as it already has in certain parts of the United States, then family life, relations between friends, and voluntary association will all be rendered two-dimensional — robbed of depth and seriousness as tough questions are passed over to paid conversationalists. A loss of confidence is already perceptible. For instance, health professionals such as doctors and nurses used, unselfconsciously, to include personal problems within their remit when circumstances seemed right and the relationship seemed appropriate. Now their capacity to do so is being undermined, and they are more likely to refer patients to specialist counsellors. Yet such counsellors are almost certainly less capable of providing helpful conversation than doctors and nurses who have more extensive background knowledge of the patient, and are likely to be better motivated and more capable individuals than the counsellors.

It is right to be inflexible on this point. There is no trainable technique for dealing with the problems of living and no routine expertise in discussing the meaning of life. Each of us must find our own path, with the help — not of paid conversationalists — but of true friends whom we know and trust, and who care about our best interests. And in the final analysis we must accept that the human condition encompasses much that cannot be cured and must be endured.

Sentimentality no substitute for taking tough decisions

The problem of that which must be endured leads on to a consideration of circumstances in which there is no ideal answer to a problem, and wanted consequences must be balanced against unwanted. Sentimentality damages the effective practice of medicine when it interferes with an ability to make *tough decisions*.

Tough decisions can be defined as decisions in which the correct course of action is obvious (to the informed and competent observer) yet in which there is nevertheless some conflict of principles, or a mixed outcome of desirable and undesirable consequences. In other words, the right answer is not the perfect answer, and every decision leaves the decider open to criticism.

On this basis most health decisions can be seen as 'tough' when they are considered in their full context; as there is seldom unmixed benefit but rather a balance of probability between help and harm. For instance, in psychiatry tough treatment decisions are frequent. There are a group of people who actively seek treatment, yet if they receive what they ask for are likely to become chronically dependent and 'addicted' to psychiatric interventions, with a severe deterioration in behaviour often including suicide attempts. The tough decision may be to resist admission and minimise contact despite the fact that these people are indeed psychiatrically ill and are asking for help. On the other hand, those psychiatric patients most likely to benefit from treatment are often insane and lack insight into their condition. To prevent harm to themselves and others, some such patients require compulsory admission and treatment. In other words, the tough decision may be to refuse hospital admission to someone who requests it, and to detain another person against his will. There are no easy answers in such circumstances, only a balance of probabilities.

Fortunately, doctors are usually rather good at making tough decisions. This is not to say that doctors always make the correct decisions, but doctors are usually equipped to be decisive without a fuss and to accept personal responsibility.[17] Indeed, doctors are perhaps more prone to make precipitate decisions, when a bit more information or time to reflect would have been helpful, than they are to shirk necessary tough decisions.

Such capacity to take responsibility is rare enough, moreover trends in health policy and society at large are undermining this. The desire to evade personal responsibility for bad outcomes yet to make a public display of concern that 'something must be done' is common among politicians, journalists and single-issue philanthropists. Using this measure of 'public opinion' as a mandate, health service managers have begun to encroach upon clinical responsibilities and to assume the power to influence clinical decisions, without accepting responsibility for the outcomes. This has initiated a shift away from the relationship of trust that ought to characterise the clinical consultation, and moved the NHS towards a reliance upon impersonal procedures such as top-down monitoring, bureaucratic regulation and the employment of explicit standards.[18] Committee solidarity takes over, and the phenomenon of group think generates flaccid compromises in place of tough decisions.

The endemic sentimentality of Western public culture is failing to support doctors in the tough decisions that they must make in the best interests of patients.[19] Unwanted consequences are bound to occur following tough decisions. This does not mean that the decision was wrong, but that intervention is never an unmixed blessing. Public policy has developed an almost hysterical obsession with safeguarding against bad outcomes — not in order to benefit the public, but in order to avoid criticism of the public policy-makers.

Decision making has become dominated by risks and neglected the *infrastructure* of good practice. Even minuscule risks, which may be purely theoretical, stand out from the background of good practice — all the more sharply because good practice has led to an expectation of uniformly good outcomes. When major surgery was genuinely dangerous, its risks were accepted, but now that the standard of surgery and anaesthesia is so very high, the occasional disaster creates much greater impact, leading to a perception of risk that is the opposite of truth. Yet, adversarial consumerism, compensation frenzy in the law courts, and the 'charter' mentality of politicians all conspire to concentrate attention upon eradicating any possibility of bad outcomes.[20] That response is inevitably to impose a regulatory system to be operated by managers who have collective power without personal responsibility.

Such sentimentality must be put on one side: a tough minded attitude is required. It is foolish to take good outcomes for granted, and the major priority of policy should be to create and sustain the infrastructure necessary for good practice.[21] In the case of medicine, a one-sided craving for risk-elimination will surely prevent the exercise of personal judgement and responsibility upon which that infrastructure depends. Bad outcomes are certain to occur in any human system, and a certain level of honest mistakes *must* be tolerated.

Bad outcomes are not invariably abuses, many are merely the workings of probability and the inevitable price that is paid for good outcomes. Drug side-effects are a case in point — therapeutic benefit is never available without side effects. Effectiveness is available only at the cost of hazard. The question is whether the balance of benefit and risk favours the patient. If we were to insist on no-risk drugs there would be no drugs.

Sentimentality: the opposite of proper medical practice

The above examples demonstrate that sentimentality is root and branch in opposition to proper medical practice. Yet because medicine is a practice, its characteristic defining *ethos* is implicit: embodied in behaviour rather than stated explicitly in a code. It will therefore be necessary to summarise imperfectly and incompletely that which is actually tacit — in part an aspiration, in part an achieved standard of practice.

Medicine is a limited activity. It has no legitimate positive role, but is concerned with the removal or amelioration of negative impediments to our proper goals. When we are well, medicine gives us a wide berth — and sensible folk do the same with medicine. Our reasoning is that health *will not last*, and the first priority should be to use what health we have in the limited time available. In other words, health is not properly an end in itself, but a means to other ends.

There are some few medical interventions which are done to prevent future disease or extend life expectation and which are applied to healthy people — immunisations, for instance. But the medical *ethos* regards such interventions as regrettable necessities, not as the defining feature of medical practice. The human mind and body are of great complexity, and it is much easier to harm health than to enhance it. Every interventional manoeuvre that does not lead to outright benefit will certainly lead to harm. Preventive medicine and health promotion are justified *only* when supported by conclusive evidence of their individually significant effectiveness, and when their inevitable disadvantages and costs are outweighed by an adequate margin of benefit. Judged by such ethical criteria, most existing instances of health promotion and preventive medicine are inappropriate.

Medicalisation is a mistaking of means for ends, it is the pursuit of health as the goal of life instead of something consumed in the pursuit of life's goals. The medical *ethos* avoids medicalisation by taking a stand on the rock of biology. Humans are vulnerable during growth and development, slow to mature, and all too soon they will decline into senescence and death. Our time is limited. To expend excessive effort on the futile task of attempting to halt the effects of time is a profound error — perhaps even a sin. As medicalisation proceeds, every life decision is permeated with a health perspective and matters of food, shelter, work, activity, sex, love, clothing may all be sucked into an outlook where their supposed health promoting qualities are the primary consideration. The goal of health becomes merely its own perpetuation.

For instance, an average human will spend approximately eight years of his life engaged in eating. Surely, it is inconceivable that such a proportion of our span should be devoted solely to a consideration of eating as a means of health promotion. (Especially given that the prevailing dietary recommendations of health promotionists are little more than a worthless fad.[22]) Eating is often the major focus of benign social intercourse and a source of great sensuous gratification. Many other competing 'goods' of life can also be pursued while eating. Those eight years might be spent actually living rather than wasted on trying to stave off death. It is irrational to sacrifice life to health.

Medicalisation is a further consequence of sentimentality; it avoids considering the contingency and brevity of human life, and at the same time makes a public fuss over attempting to delay the inevitable. But the human condition is intractable. Health must be enjoyed while it lasts because, whether we like it or not, health is burned up in living.

Realism in medical practice: the antidote to sentimentality
As a student doctor I was taught 'no reassurance without explanation'. These wise words sum up the case against sentimentality in medicine. When the chips are down we should not reach for emotional placebos; an attitude of realism ought to be the default position. This is not to excuse harshness or ill manners. Good nature is rightly prized in a physician, but the temptations for patients to deny unpleasant factors or for doctors to 'fob-off' patients with anodynes need to be resisted.

Doctors are not naturally sentimental beings; far from it. Left to their own devices, away from patients and behind closed doors, doctors indulge in 'gallows' humour. Medical students and newly-qualified doctors are ghoulishly cynical, employing crude and flippant slang to depersonalise the horrors of the human condition. This pose of icy, sarcastic disdain is — fortunately — a temporary phase, probably produced as a side effect of overwork, rigid hierarchical surveillance and barrack-like conditions.

But when a doctor acquiesces in sentimental evasion, *this* is when alarm bells should ring. When sentimentality intrudes into medicine, we can be confident that charlatanry is seldom far behind. Sentimentality is an effective cloak for evasive waffle and covert exploitation. When a patient refuses to accept realistic advice from a responsible doctor, he is driven by inevitable degrees into the hands of unscrupulous quacks who are delighted to take the money and lather him with lashings of soft soap.

Medicine cannot guarantee happy endings; these only happen in fairy tales of the worst sort. Life is often unfair, and many people do not obtain their just deserts. The only true answer to the question so often asked by the afflicted — 'Why me?' — is that, biologically speaking, it is health which is rare and extraordinary, and disease and death that are the norm.[23]

The best doctors are exactly those who eschew sentimentality and enable the patient to 'master' his condition through providing explanations that are clear, meaningful, hopeful and honest. The wise physician will not seek reassurance at any price, but will, by his example, bring the patient to confront reality with hope and fortitude; the doctor remaining (as it were) by the patient's side, showing that it is sometimes possible to stare death and disease in the face without being overwhelmed.

> So large a part of human life passes in a state contrary to our natural desires that one of the principal topics of moral instruction is the art of bearing calamities. And such is the certainty of evil that it is the duty of every man to furnish his mind with those principles that may enable him to act under it with decency and propriety.
>
> *Samuel Johnson,* The Rambler, *Number 32*

Acknowledgement: Thanks to Dr Gillian Rye for many helpful comments and advice during the writing of this chapter.

3

Evading personal responsibility

the sentimentalisation of social policy

Nicholas Capaldi

An example

In March 1997, in a large city in the north-eastern part of the United States, a tragic fire occurred. Three children died in a fire in *slum* housing. The fire was caused by the malfunctioning of a space heater. Space heaters had long been outlawed by the municipality precisely because their operation is subject to risks. Why then did the adult occupants employ such a heater? They used the space heater because the landlord did not provide *adequate* heating.

As this story was reported in the media, the responsibility for this tragic event was attributed to the landlord, dubbed a 'slumlord'. The mother of the deceased children became an object of public compassion. As the story unfolded, we were told that the mother deserved this public solicitude because she was an African American, had three remaining children (a total at one time of six — birth certificates indicated four different fathers), was unmarried (had in fact never been married), and was receiving public assistance (welfare).

Sentimentality blames external forces for lapses in personal responsibility

The conceptualisation of this event may be summarised as follows. *First level*: all tragedy is in principle eliminable from social life. Hence, it must always be possible to affix responsibility for tragic events. The 'slumlord' is the immediate guilty party because he failed to provide adequate heating. If we probe deeper we find that the 'slumlord' provides substandard housing at below market prices. People choose to live in substandard housing because it is cheaper. If the 'slumlord' had provided adequate (standard) housing at market prices, the occupants would have opted to live in substandard housing elsewhere. *Second level*: the public assistance agencies (and ultimately the public at large) are responsible because they fail to provide an adequate allowance for standard housing. If we probe deeper we find that the sum total of public assistance financing for a single mother with six dependent children is sufficient to support adequate housing if the sum total of the welfare funds was properly managed.

Third level: the public is responsible for failing to take the total economic situation into account. No welfare recipient with dependent children can be expected to manage on current public assistance allowances. To take but one example, children apparently *need* expensive and fashionable athletic shoes in order to have a decent life. Generalising this point, there is a standard of living defined by whatever is the current level of the middle class such that all children need this level in order to grow into functional adults. The children need and deserve this level of subsistence no matter what the condition of the parents may be. If we were to probe deeper, we would discover that the subsistence level of current welfare recipients, adjusted even for inflation, in 1997 is higher than the income of middle class Americans was in 1955. Most of the children of those Americans managed to become responsible and functional adults without expensive and fashionable athletic shoes or their counterparts.

Fourth level: it is, however, unfair to compare current unmarried African American female heads of household with dependent children to typical American families of the 1950s. The whole of the past history of the United States, or the United States as a collective historic entity, is responsible through slavery, Jim Crow discrimination and ongoing racism, for creating a class of people who at the very least do not consistently instantiate the virtuous practices (eg, getting married, limiting family size commensurate with income, postponing gratification, etc) of the middle class. Unwed teenagers become pregnant because they either do not know what causes pregnancy; or do not know how to use any form of birth control (celibacy is an unreasonable demand to make on victims of racism, etc); or cannot afford birth control materials; or are so starved for affection and attention that having a child to love is something to be welcomed. All of this could have been avoided if public assistance had properly funded sex education in the schools and provided free birth control assistance. This, of course, echoes the third level. Probing deeper, however, we find that there are and have been many African Americans who, under the same set of circumstances, have developed into members of the middle class and some of whom have become social leaders.

Fifth level: the historical-social process from slavery through Jim Crow segregation to racism is 'a' if not 'the' cause of all of the social problems that afflict African Americans. We may not know the exact process of how this takes place in some but not all African Americans but that is because not enough public and private foundation money has been spent subsidising the research of social scientists. *Nth level*: no matter what, there is always some external social or subtle internal psychological force that is ultimately responsible for why bad things happen to people. The individuals are never under any set of circumstances responsible. Even the subtle internal psychological forces are ultimately the product of external social forces. It is never necessary for bad things to happen; all tragedy is in principle eliminable, and that is why we should be sympathetic with each and every sociopath.

The logic of sentimentality

Sentimentality, as the *Oxford English Dictionary* tells us, is the exaggerated insistence upon the claims of sentiment. A sentiment is a thought coloured by or proceeding from an emotion and therefore expressive of an attitude of approval or disapproval. The expression of sentiment is exaggerated when it insists emotionally upon a regard to ideal considerations as a principle of judgement or action.

What are the ideal considerations that currently infect sentimentality in public policy? There are four: Pelagianism; utopianism; secularism; and the liberal paradigm. It is the concatenation of these four considerations, culminating in the liberal paradigm, that has permitted sentimentality to serve as a substitute for morality.

Sentimentality denies the psychological reality of Original Sin

Sentimentality is a perversion of Christianity. Specifically, sentimentality is *Pelagian*. Pelagius was a fifth-century British monk who both denied the doctrine of Original Sin and affirmed that our free will was sufficient to allow us to save ourselves. Unlike his rival, St Augustine, Pelagius believed that it was possible to achieve perfection in this life and to live without sinning. In the terminology of Eric Voegelin, Pelagianism is a form of *gnosticism* in maintaining the immanentisation of the eschaton.[1]

The denial of the doctrine of Original Sin is of fundamental importance. The constant tension in Western civilisation has been between those who think that salvation is possible in this life (utopianism) and those who deny it. Sentimentality is an inevitable by-product of the former. It is, therefore, important to review what adherents of sentimental utopia oppose.

What Pelagianism denies is the classical Christian Western conception of the cosmos. First, that there is a cosmic order that is divinely created. Secondly, human beings possess the rational capacity to recognise the universal moral truths embedded in that cosmic order. Thirdly, human beings have the internal capacity to be unconstrained in their decision to act in accordance with the universal truth, ie *free will*. Fourthly, although human beings have free will, they almost invariably allow themselves to be governed by their base passions.

The drive for self-assertion

Furthermore, *sin* is the fact that human beings are born with a fundamental drive for self-assertion. This is exemplified in the child's crying to demand nourishment and attention. This self-assertion may have a certain survival value but it is also the origin of our self-destructive impulses, our desire to have things or do things in response to immediate impulse that we know could destroy us in the long run. From a social point of view, self-assertion is destructive since it leads inevitably to the clash of wills. These self-destructive impulses can only be overcome by conscious self-discipline.

The capacity of self-discipline requires a supportive social environment but it also requires God's grace. Without God's grace we lack as individuals the capacity to resist temptation. We need to appeal to a force greater than ourselves and external to ourselves to help us to gain internal control of our lives. The social environment is supportive only to the extent that it encourages individuals to learn both about their shortcomings and their strengths; in order for our strengths ultimately to come into play requires recognition of something greater than and more important than ourselves. The paradox is that we seem to be both free and not free at the same time. St Augustine resolved this paradox by maintaining that we are free to accept God's grace but without that acceptance we shall lack the power to overcome our base impulses. The importance of some conception of grace has an analogue in the 12-step programme that addicts use to deal with their addiction.

Finally, true freedom and dignity consist in the inner or self-discipline that comes with the exercise of these capacities. These capacities can only be discovered retrospectively by their exercise. The upshot of this conception is that *the freedom and dignity of responsible autonomy cannot be understood except by those who exercise it*, that the self-discipline to exercise it cannot be mechanically induced from the outside and that even the exercise of our rational capacity is a matter of self-discipline. The choice to use one's reason and to use it to the fullest extent, to pursue the argument to its logical conclusion and not merely to the convenient conclusion is not made by reason but by an inner act of self-discipline.

Anti-social behaviour is the natural result of a lack of self-discipline. Self-discipline is learned behaviour but it is not totally induced from the outside, because while outside example and support is important, the final result depends upon free will; and in order to make people whole, we must provide them not only with good examples (ie, examples of self-discipline) but also with opportunities to learn in an internal sense self-control and personal responsibility by holding them responsible for what they do. This is not a political or technical task but a moral one. Notice that this does not deny the importance of environmental influence but it does stress that there is something more fundamental than the environment, namely human free will, and it has a different conception of what constitutes a benign environment. This is not a call for inaction but for action; however, it denies that there is a guaranteed utopian resolution of the human predicament.

What Pelagianism does is to eliminate the notion that sin is basic. Human beings are fundamentally good and can of their own free will and without grace come to accept and abide by God's cosmic order. What the Pelagian heresy amounts to for us is the denial of sin and the insistence upon the fundamental goodness of human nature. In the classical and medieval world, gnostic utopianism was sought in the exercise of techniques that allegedly released us from the body. When we turn to the modern world, we see that gnosticism took a new form.

The Enlightenment Project substituted politics for morality

The Enlightenment Project[2] was the attempt to define, explain, and control the human predicament through science and technology. The Enlightenment Project appealed to an autonomous human reason, freed of any higher authority and channelled itself through science as its privileged tool. There is still a belief in a cosmic order, but not a divinely created one. The cosmic order is to be accessed through science. This project originated among the French *philosophes* during the eighteenth century, among whom the most influential were Diderot, d'Alembert, La Mettrie, Condillac, Helvétius, d'Holbach, Turgot and Condorcet. The *philosophes* were inspired by Bacon's vision of the liberating power of science, Hobbes's materialism, Newton's physics, and Locke's empiricist epistemology. The Project was epitomised in the nineteenth century by Comte and in the twentieth by positivism.

The Enlightenment Project is a modern form of gnosticism, only now the gnosticism is a form of materialism. We are nothing but our bodies, and our bodies can be manipulated to achieve utopian results. Specifically, the conception of moral and political philosophy that emanates from the Enlightenment Project is the idea of social engineering or social technology. By *social engineering* is meant the following: first, the conceptualisation of the human situation not as a condition or predicament but as a set of problems, such as the problems of poverty, racism, anxiety, depression, crime, unemployment, teenage pregnancy, war, etc; secondly, the belief that there can be an objective social scientific consensus on what these problems are; thirdly, the belief that the origin of these problems lies not in human nature or in the human predicament but in physical, environmental, or institutional structures; fourthly, the belief that to each problem there is a solution; fifthly, the utopian belief that unique technical solutions can be found, at some level, that do not themselves create new or additional unsolvable problems or that do not conflict irremediably with the solution to other problems; and finally, the belief that the solution always involves reconstructing the physical, environmental, or institutional structures. For example, the response to crime might be either genetic engineering, or adding more psychologists to elementary education programmes, or improving diets in school lunches, or more prisons and police, or a planned economy guaranteeing a job. As this example is intended to show, representatives of different places on the political spectrum can still all nevertheless subscribe to a general belief in social engineering or technology.

A changed notion of freedom and the rise of feeling
Changes in the meaning of the concept of 'freedom' help to explain the substitution of politics for morality. As materialists, modern gnostics deny the radical freedom of the will and opt instead for some form of determinism. Freedom is compatible with determinism only if *freedom is construed as the absence of external constraints*. By subscribing to internal determinism, *no distinction exists between 'freedom' and 'liberty'*.

These terms refer interchangeably to environmental constraints. Statist social programmes make us free if they remove external constraints; the more powerful the government becomes in order to remove restraints the more 'free' it makes us. This paradoxical conception of freedom leads to *a political conception of ethics based on external social sanctions instead of morality (which involves the inner sanction of autonomous agents)*.

A further consequence of the Enlightenment Project is the rise of the 'man of feeling'. If morality is to have a natural empirical and scientific base, then morality becomes identified with our moral feelings. However, under the aegis of the Enlightenment Project, instead of deep feelings about the violation of moral principles, the man of feeling made how deeply we feel the basis for moral principle. Of course, these new feelings were informed by the belief about the natural goodness of human beings. Christian charity informed by principle was displaced by the depth of distress at another's misfortune. These new men of feeling became the object of scorn by noted eighteenth-century writers such as Samuel Johnson and Edmund Burke.

Sentimentality generates the impulse to engage in social engineering

The *liberal paradigm* is a framework for conceptualising public policy, and it is the contemporary expression of the Enlightenment Project. It is a paradigm in the Kuhnian sense of structuring how people respond to facts and experience. It is a pervasive paradigm that currently dominates the academy, the media, and even much of religion. Recognising this framework as a paradigm should help us to understand why those who oppose it are greeted with disbelief and revulsion.

Consider the following analogy. Imagine an aeroplane with 100 seats, 50 on each side of a central aisle. Imagine that 40 passengers become violently ill on one flight. Imagine that of the ill passengers, 30 are seated on the left of the aisle and 10 are seated on the right of the aisle. Someone suggests that sitting on the left side of an aeroplane must cause a greater degree of motion sickness even though no engineering study can confirm this. On the other hand, someone else calls attention to the fact that the 40 ill passengers chose the steak dinner, while all the other passengers chose the chicken dinner. Is it not more reasonable to suspect food poisoning than position on the aircraft? The proponents of affirmative action and supporters of the liberal paradigm are like those who keep calling attention to the fact that most of the sick people sat on the left side of the plane.

The liberal paradigm makes the following assumptions: first, human beings are born with impulses that are basically good (the denial of the traditional Christian doctrine of Original Sin); secondly, all anti-social behaviour is the result of external environmental influence (eg, lack of information or resources, presence of hostile attitudes and the absence of approving attitudes); and thirdly, in order to make people whole again, it is necessary to engage in social engineering or the reconstruction of institutions so as to provide information and resources, eliminate hostile attitudes, and promote approving attitudes.

Given this paradigm, how do people respond to the failure of, let us say, African Americans, to participate fully in American life? Almost all anti-social behaviour on the part of African Americans is excused as due to ignorance, poverty, and racism on the part of the rest of society. The suggested solution is more and better education (ie, opposing segregated schools even when the resources available are the same, advocating bussing and lowering admission standards so that African Americans can move more rapidly to the next educational level), increasing resources (ie, higher welfare expenditure, raising the minimum wage, the hiring, training, and promoting of African Americans more rapidly than past performance warrants, and contract set-asides), and, finally, eliminating or muting hostile attitudes toward African Americans (ie, increasing contact among the races in schools and elsewhere, promoting role models, increasing the presence of African Americans in advertisements, producing a stream of works of literature and film that invariably depict African Americans as victims, constantly reminding us that those who oppose these policies and the liberal paradigm in general are contributing to the hostile environment, constantly rehearsing public reaffirmations of solidarity with oppressed peoples, and supporting just about any programme that is well intentioned or designed to put the liberal paradigm into practice no matter how flimsy the support). What is frequently identified as 'liberal guilt' might be more aptly described as continual efforts to do something, to implement the paradigm, even in the face of the failure and counter-productivity of all previous efforts. As Shelby Steele has pointed out:

> Affirmative action has always been...iconographic public policy
> — policy that ostensibly exists to solve social problems but actually

functions as an icon for the self-image people hope to gain by supporting the policy. From the beginning, affirmative action could be cited as evidence of White social virtue.[3]

Love redefined as politics

How do those who reject the liberal paradigm respond to the predicament of African Americans? Fundamentally there is the opposition to the rhetoric of victimisation. This is not to deny past history or even its relevance, but rather to stress that what is most important is to take personal responsibility. The rhetoric of victimisation (I call it 'rhetoric' because it is not a hypothesis that has scientific support) seeks to explain what happens to African Americans totally in terms of larger social forces without due consideration to the moral response of individuals. This rhetoric has become the great alibi. Further, there is opposition to granting special privileges (which is what affirmative action as preference is all about) precisely because you cannot learn self-discipline by having things made easier.

> The fundamental problem with this form of affirmative action is the way it leaps over the hard business of developing a formerly oppressed people to the point where they can achieve proportionate representation on their own (given equal opportunity) and goes straight for the proportionate re-presentation. This may satisfy some whites of their innocence and some blacks of their power. But it does very little to truly uplift blacks...The old sin is reaffirmed in a new guise.[4]

Self-respect, which is what African Americans need in order to participate fully, comes from the inside, it comes from what an individual does for himself or herself. Given what I have said about the historical connection between Christianity and responsible individuality, it is no accident that the most stable institution among African Americans has been religion. Self-respect is not to be confused with self-esteem, which comes from the recognition of others, and it is not to be confused with either false bravado or delusions of grandeur. Ernest van den Haag notes,

> Groups of Negroes may profit: Negroes as a group will suffer. Their self-image of inferiority to whites and of inadequacy will be reinforced. And the white's image of Negroes as inferior, as less well qualified for most things than whites, will be confirmed.[5]

49

Crucially important in the opposition to the liberal paradigm is the role of families. The family is the central institution where we learn self-discipline, generally because it is within the family that a special bond of affection exists that allows for the self-disclosure that expresses the need for change so necessary for self-critique and self-discipline. Any public policy that undermines families, no matter how well intentioned, undercuts any attempt to provide the conditions within which African Americans can come to participate fully. Unfortunately, affirmative action is part and parcel of all those forms of social engineering that have as an inadvertent consequence the weakening of family life. The increasing threat to the family is its loss of function as more and more is taken over by public agencies who thus compete for the attention and esteem of children.

Responding to adversity

The question is not whether any of us will experience hostility in our lives but how we respond to the hostility, and how we respond reflects in part our sense of self. Nathan Glazer says,

> Some groups — even those bearing the badge of discrimination — have achieved more than equality... To label [discrimination] as the cause of the economic differences between groups, even when it is extensive and pervasive, is a gross oversimplification.[6]

I am not 'blaming the victim' but calling attention to a different contextual explanation. But it is also true that the problem can never be solved by blaming the perpetrators of slavery or calling attention to conditions that no longer exist.

Under the liberal paradigm, government policies failed to promote the sense of personal responsibility. I hasten to add that this factor is not a particular social structure but the failure to promote or encourage a change in psychological makeup; wherever individualism was allowed to flourish, many African Americans were able to participate to a remarkable degree despite public policies.

Although the liberal paradigm is secular and even in its origin anti-theistic, it has penetrated deeply into contemporary liberal Protestantism.[7] At the risk of gross over-simplification, we maintain that liberal Protestantism sought to maintain a close connection between Christianity and the dominant wider secular culture. Anglican Protestantism, traditional Catholics, conservative Protestants and evangelical Protestants remain critics of that dominant wider culture.

The result is that within liberal Protestant denominations, traditional Christian concepts such as love and charity have been transformed by notions of social justice. Most important of all, Rousseau's notion of the natural goodness of human nature has turned these denominations in the Pelagian direction.

The human predicament is that utopian, sentimental solutions are simply not to be had

Sentimentality has become a substitute for morality. Real life moral dilemmas consist of choices not between good and evil (that's too easy to resolve) but between two evils. The existence of that kind of world is precisely what advocates of sentimentality cannot face. Sentimentality reflects the decline of the Judeo-Christian tradition. It is a by-product of the current domination of the cultural and intellectual elite by the liberal paradigm, a process that started in the French Enlightenment Project. At the same time, we contend that the basic roots even of the Enlightenment Project are ultimately gnostic and Pelagian. Sentimentality will disappear but only to have its place taken by other forms of gnosticism. This is not a problem to be solved, for the irrepressible desire to conceive of the human predicament as having a utopian resolution is itself a reflection of the true human predicament, the lived experience of dealing with conflicts that have no utopian this-worldly resolution.

4

Sweetness and light in schools
the sentimentalisation of children

Bruce S Cooper and Dennis O'Keeffe

Introduction: indulging children

Anxieties about education in the United States and Great Britain have, over the years, focused on a huge range of factors. This chapter takes its stance on the cognitive and moral side. We hold that education has been failing because a wrong understanding of what education is has been widely institutionalised in schools and colleges. Strange attitudes and protocols have taken hold, ousting reason and evidence. These shape the structure and funding of schools: they pervade the curriculum and pedagogy; they influence, adversely, the standards and deportment of pupils; and they have an enfeebling effect on the assessment of competence.

The strange attitudes have many names. The most compendious is 'sentimentality'. What is sentimentality? Philosophical characterisation is not hard, despite the lack of academic interest so far. Scruton defines sentimentality, stipulatively, as the process whereby the subject of contemplation is substituted for its object.[1] Applied to people, sentimentality treats them as the means with which to gratify feelings (sentiments) treated as ends. Those who sentimentalise are mostly self-serving. Sentimentality thus offends against the Kantian imperative.

Sentimentalists romanticise childhood, ostensibly proclaiming the natural goodness of children, but in fact pandering to human idleness. As the work ethic has collapsed in schools, childhood has lost its proper place in the development of adulthood. This sugary ideology also shapes the preparation of teachers, dominating their induction as beginners. It is also constantly revivified in their subsequent careers. The sentimental ascendancy is so strong that any contrary view of the mushy ambience of college or school, is met with real or simulated outrage, and stigmatised as disloyalty to the dream of state education.

Today's ignorance reflects moral and intellectual confusion. We are harangued by moralisms and assailed by technicist conceits. 'Our goodness is rotted by a cruel world', say the 'experts'. 'It's all someone's fault. We have the know-how to fix it, if the state coughs up enough money, though of course it's all hopeless anyway.' This mix of despair and managerial hubris defines the 'modern' mind-set of education, bemused, like all socialist fantasy, with fugitive, incompatible and incredible solutions.

The error which bonds together this unstable compound is sentimentality. If five per cent of the research done on 'racism' or 'sexism' recently had been committed to understanding folly of the sentimental type, we would have a much better grasp of what is wrong with education.

Has sentimentality no place ever? Perhaps it has. Where it merges with functional hypocrisy it may sometimes be right. Clearly it can be a comfort at weddings and positively stirring on birthdays. At funerals too, a tactful hypocrisy may govern proceedings. On such occasions sentimentality constitutes, no doubt, a politic diplomacy, covering up individual shortcomings and fractured relationships, as well as the risks and uncertainties marring all family life.[2]

Sentimentality could not be routinely wholesome in our domestic lives, however. To work well, the family, like any moral agency, must evaluate life with uncompromising ruthlessness. If sentimentality makes a brief appearance at weddings, birthdays and funerals, this is a temporary suspension of normal reality for the sake of other aspects of family and friendship.

Sentimentality has no comparable claim on education. A public agency — at any rate a fundamentally *intellectual* one — cannot decently sustain, or not often, an emotionalism of the kind a private agency like the family sometimes actually *demands*. What is just about permissible *in extremis* in the latter, is a cloying irrelevance in the former.

Sentimentality is a general modern error, widely instantiated. Beyond the mistake in Kantian terms Scruton identifies, what else is it? In the next section we analyse the concept and its context in some detail, before returning in later sections to its educational manifestations.

Sentimentality: childish, mawkish, bogus?

Our more elaborate definitional foray takes an adjectival focus, as we look for words broadly cognate with 'sentimental', or, more ambitiously, for actual synonyms.

There are many cognates of sentimentality, some obvious like 'childish', 'infantilising', 'maudlin', 'mawkish', 'insecure', 'bogus', 'fake', 'fraudulent' and 'saccharine'. (These are without doubt useful for tracking down sentimental education.) The phrase 'chocolate box', used metaphorically, is a very sharp guide to sentimentality, catching an overdone sweetness both of taste and visual image. Sentimentality is a false sweetness camouflaging the often bitter facts of the world.

Synonyms are more difficult, with no obvious one despite pervasive sentimentality. Nor have we a substantial critical history of 'the sentimental'. This suggests it is a novel phenomenon. Critics like Jane Austen[3] and Stendhal[4] get to it only in its fairly early stages. Yet to those who believe in human nature, the ubiquity of the sentimental today suggests strongly that it cannot be wholly new. It must have some abiding connection with the original set of moral errors at the core of human waywardness.

True, many *factors* which today fortify sentimentality are new. They are the modern scaffolding around a monumental fault. Error has homed in advisedly on vulnerable new institutions lying conveniently to hand: mass communication systems, especially mass education. The phenomenological newness of sentimentality reflects the novelty of these. Putting it formally, we may say that the ontological core of sentimentality — which may sustain many other realised faults — is a datum of human history, while its phenomenological realisation depends on variable contingencies within that history.

One reason scholarship has thus far not pinned down sentimentality's adverse effects is that we do not properly understand the new institutions. The worst gap is the educational one. Our knowledge of mass education systems is quite inadequate. Modern sociology of education, having languished under neo-Marxism for decades,[5] now declines, too often, under an even more sterile sub-Political Correctness. As for Media Studies, which should enlighten us about how the mass media actually work, the subject is today even more cravenly given over to the new, sentimental obsessions.[6]

If we are right that the roots of the sentimental reach down into our ancient depths, such that its apparent newness is radically misleading, of which sin is it the new, contingent guise?

Pride is the answer. The sentimentality of the present West is, essentially, a manifestation of our old prideful disposition to wrong belief. For many complex reasons, the tendency of fanciful human beings to seek to rewrite reality — to adhere to perverse understandings of the world — often takes the form we now call sentimentality.

Perversity has assimilated itself to new circumstances. Above all, this ingenious adaptation of ill has run rather ahead of corrective understanding. Educational researchers, instead of concentrating on civilisational issues — knowledge and morals — have been obsessed with secondary issues of power and equality, very often viewed through the flawed prism of sentimentality.

Whatever happened to criticism?

References to sentimentality in intellectual history are very scanty. The phenomenon has grown in the absence of philosophical correction. Interestingly, however, Arthur Koestler linked it with aggression, seeing in the union of the two the besetting sin of modern Germany.[7] Sentimentality is clearly a major component of many ills: of terrorism, for example,[8] and of totalitarianism in all its guises.[9]

Shakespeare was not talking about sentimentality, but easily could have been, when he spoke of those who commit the oldest kind of sin the newest kind of way.[10] Sentimentality is this sort of ancient/modern error. Its first influential prophet was Rousseau. His fateful influence has run in an unbroken chain through the Romantic tradition, rebuking the rationalism of the Enlightenment. Modern radical ideology has roots in both; but Romanticism is the definitive presence, as Finkielkraut makes clear.[11] Nowhere is this more apparent in the free societies than in education.

What is sentimentality like?

Like all Pharisaical evasion, educational sentimentality requires a certain cover. This explains the addiction to ideological abstractions such as 'empowerment' and the 'owning' of knowledge or morals. Revealingly, their proponents never give us any real sense of what they mean. Sentimentality is likewise hostile to evidence, not from a healthy concept for much so-called empirical social scientific research — who could help but agree? — but from its hatred of reality. Reality is too stark in some ways, too complex and finely nuanced in others, to appeal to the unrigorous or dishonest mind.

To denounce sentimentality is not to decry our affective lives. We could not function without our feelings. We are redeemed through the modification of our intellects by our sentiments, and vice versa. People who seem like desiccated calculating machines have simply not had their cold logical powers modified by pity or empathy. Civilised behaviour is a kind of rationally refined feeling, which, rather than logic itself, leads us to treat people as ends and not means.

Other influences on sentimentality

There are other, auxiliary influences on sentimentality, certain novel facts like our new longevity and amazing affluence. The mechanics of life have a new-found ease, one which has assumed an educational aspect. Academic life, too, is now increasingly soft and undemanding. There is also a decline in religious conviction. Faith has been replaced, however, not by a tough, all round scepticism, but by a sentimental credulity. Lots of seemingly sensible people, for example, now believe in ideas like the innate goodness of children, a notion our grandparents would have thought absurd.[12] The instinct to engage in religion has not died, merely latched on to surrogates and caricatures of belief, such as the weird modern addiction to bogus atonement. This is so deeply tinged by Pharisaism and self-regard as to resemble, very closely, sentimentality itself. In institutions of learning, especially, the impulse to offer insincere repentance, for 'transgressors' to identify themselves and their 'victims' and enact strange rituals and services of sorrow,[13] reveals the operations of a guilt culture that has lost its bearings, and in particular lost the knack of determining accurately who is guilty of what and why. Why on earth should people labelled 'middle class' feel guilty about others labelled 'working class' for example? Precisely this mawkish thinking informs much of what goes on in the education, welfare and legal services today.[14]

There is also our practice, probably well-intentioned at first but now provenly disastrous, of committing the cognitive and moral instruction of the young to lavishly-funded public institutions, whose personnel, however, never stop pleading lack of funds. Publicly-funded mass schooling has proved wholly inadequate.[15] It is not competitive enough and it is too liable to ideological subversion, as its addiction to sentimentality shows.

Behind the talk about children born good and subverted by a 'corrupt' society lies a very grim story. A meaningless virtue is attributed to pre-moral infancy, but as the child gets older a sinister blankness is imposed on his or her moral nature. Our culture maintains a saccharine rendition of childhood. Just where moral discretion should begin, however, when boys and girls are old enough to sustain serious blame for their misdeeds, they are made the objects of determinist understandings of their condition and the sense of their human agency is profoundly weakened.[16]

Life's likely losers are turned into near-inevitable failures. To see which group has been worst hit by bogus charity, we need only observe which lot are seen as least human by the sentimentalist. As with all socialist ideology, which is what sentimentality is when it is publicly financed, it is the weak who get hurt most. It is heartbreaking to contemplate the web of debilitating condescension woven pre-emptively through their lives. If social science has taught us anything, however, it is that people tend to act as they are defined. The vile behaviour of many young people, in and out of school, is partly caused by the contempt heaped on them. The insults also work *post hoc* as sentimental justifications, people's misdeeds being insultingly explained away by their poverty, housing, race, and unemployment, or by the alleged unwillingness of governments to fund their lives more lavishly.[17]

This brings us back to pride. Only a very proud soul will conceive others as lacking all moral powers. Many of today's Pharisees constantly reinforce that pride by recourse to sentimental reasoning, especially by resorting to determinist and dehumanising understandings of the human condition, in the face of an accumulating evidence against any such purely materialist theses.[18] Whatever the reason, certain groups of people, occupying key points in our civilisation — especially in school but also in law and welfare — often demand that reality be blotted out. The main way of achieving this is to pull a curtain of sentimentality across anything they do not want to face. A vacuous optimism sits alongside determinism. Many adults now flee from the fact that children are stormy, dangerous instinct-systems, little egotists not likely to reach their marvellous potential without proper moral and intellectual guidance, including periodic punishment for infractions of moral and other rules. It is a direct result of sentimentality that so many adults, instead of feeling responsible for helping wayward children, and genuinely bound to guide them in better ways, either affect guilt or sorrow for them, in terms of the factors allegedly 'causing' their shortcomings, or pretend the children have none.

The form taken by sentimentality in school: the deriding of discipline and obedience

We are not such fools as to suggest that American and British schools are a very wicked version of the sentimental error. After all, we live in a century during which wholly untenable ideas of race and class have exerted a murderous effect on countless millions of human beings. In this league of wrong-doing the education systems of the free societies are only very amateur offenders.

Even so, things are very bad. In recent decades, in both America and Britain, education has set aside discipline and obedience, and replaced them with false love and slackness. This is the defining error of our educational practice. The educational version is far from the only Anglo-American expression of the vice; but it is the most significant one, since education purports to make public the highest values held by a society — those it deems worthy of transmission and reproduction. If sentimentality once pervades education, it will in time pervade everything else.

Sentimentalising childhood means you do not have to deal with real children, with their idleness, selfishness and potential for violence. Instead you talk cant about unspoilt young natures. Sentimentalising the needs of children in the abstract you can neglect their real, concrete needs — for order and secure moral boundaries.

Values have to be taught

The conceptual structure of progressive thinking is very thin, really only a sketchy philosophical psychology. We should not, say the progressives, impose middle-class values on people for whom they are not appropriate. We have, accordingly, witnessed the imposition on millions of children of the outlandish views on parenting and school of a very unrepresentative segment of the middle class. Most middle-class homes are strict, which is how they maintain their solidity and affluence. 'Not imposing middle-class values' is the cant of an irresponsible minority.

Progressivism contradicts what most middle-class people do with their children. In most private schools, children are certainly not allowed to speak freely in class, or walk about as they choose. The idea that they should be allowed to do so, widely imposed on the masses in primary schools for 40 years, must also have been utterly alien to the experience of most working-class parents when they first met them. These oddities are the sentimental fancies of a middle-class *segment* which selectively abstracts from certain truths about middle-class order — the deep care which went with it, even when it was very strict — and then imposes a shallow version of this on children for whom it is often particularly inappropriate. All children need order, those from disordered homes especially.

Sentimentality has been very successful. It has slipped out of its educational confines and colonised parenting. 'Progressivism' is probably now even more typical of home than classrooms, with many parents wanting school to impose an order they do not supply at home. This sentimentalising of the world now forms a barrier to civilised learning which would take years to dismantle even if we were sure how to do it, which we are not.

The self-image of this group of busybodies, as kind and worldly-wise persons, has displaced the real interest of children as a focus of concern. The history of progressive education is a sentimental story extraordinary, involving a sustained and perverse displacement of known and well tried facts about children by the fake, self-righteous feelings of the displacers.

It must not be imagined that sentimentality is merely kindness gone wrong. Scruton has also most astutely scotched the notion that sentimentality has kind motives. His words are directed at those who sentimentalise over animals; but much the same reflection applies to those whose false charity pretends to lavish care on children:

> The sentimentalising and "kitschification" of pets may seem to many the epitome of kind-heartedness. In fact it is very often the opposite: a way of enjoying the luxury of warm emotions without the usual cost of feeling them, a way of targeting an innocent victim with simulated love which it lacks the understanding to reject or criticise, and of confirming thereby a habit of heartlessness.[19]

We can make direct educational application of the suggestion that the sentimentalist prizes his own feelings of virtue at the expense of the objects of his contemplation. The sentimental educator ill-treats children — proposes or secures wrong management of their learning and instruction, in defiance of tried and trusted reason and experience — in ways which flatter his pride, his glow of self-righteousness.

Children are infinitely more important than animals and also by definition vastly stronger cognitively; but they are weaker and less experienced than adults. Few children understand the pride and falsity which lie behind the slackness of so much modern schooling. Students preparing to be teachers often do; but we hear surprisingly little from that source.

Why should this be? Are all trainee teachers convinced progressives?

No; but terrible anger and ruthlessness are directed against anyone daring to challenge the 'consensus'. The worst bullies of our education are notable both for the peacock pride with which they maintain what they think is virtue, and for their vengeful retaliation if they are ever crossed by weaker parties. Some of them are very well known. Their faces are often on television and their articles appear in the quality newspapers. They tend to hate our civilisation, to despise America and Britain. On the other hand, they fanatically defend our education system and its ideologies.

Why do educators become sentimentalists? Pride and careless thinking

Since the sentimentality of school is so widespread, and since most people in education can scarcely be thought stupid, there must be a disabling trap into which people fall easily. There is: the union of pride and careless thinking. We need wisdom and instruction from those wiser than we, if we are to avoid sentimentality. Error can lead us astray precisely because of our desire to think well both of ourselves and of others. If we switch Scruton's analysis from the sentimentalising of animals to that of children, we can see how the unwary go wrong. The sentimental approach to the young is easy to mistake for real care for their welfare, since both seem directed at children and both seem guided by the importance of their education.

The similarity is superficial, however. Tradition holds that during their childhood we must teach children what is good. Other things being equal, the old are wiser than the young. For the first 80 years or so of its existence in America and Britain, that new phenomenon, mass education, took precisely this view. It has been only in the last half century that there have been enough 'progressives' for their claims to make headway. We know their mantras now. We should not 'steal' children's childhood. We should let them find out things for themselves. Children must 'own' their knowledge and morals, and this can happen only if they 'explore' and 'negotiate' the cognitive and moral issues in question for themselves.

Sentimentality is incorrigibly vague. What does it mean to 'own' a moral belief? Does it mean a child thinks the belief true? Or that he or she knows that it *is* true? If the latter is the case, the Jesuits are surely right. How, moreover, does one 'negotiate' a sense of revulsion for theft, violence or cruelty? What is there to be negotiated? Might victims of rape, now perpetrated, terrifyingly, by ever younger children, have been spared if their rapists had 'made the prohibition their own'? Let no one doubt the power of sentimentality. Teacher education in America and Britain is notable for its lack of a sizeable conservative presence. Here we speak from personal knowledge. It is generally difficult for trainees to maintain any kind of conservative position during their preparation and often difficult for them, once teaching, to rise in the job if they oppose the sentimental orthodoxy.

Sentimentality is often the parasite of truth: real love means knowing children for what they are

Like many errors, sentimentality preys on love. The love of adults for children is integral to civilisation. Progressivism is false love, love for the contemplator and not for the object (the child) under contemplation. To help children become decent people we must maintain a ruthless clarity in their regard. Real love means knowing children for what they are, bad points as much as good.

Children at school are still children. They deserve kindness, care, encouragement and support. Yet they must also be treated professionally and with equanimity by their teachers, if they are to become balanced, hardworking and well-educated adults. No one thinking of their good could possibly suggest a light disciplinary regime. Such a proposal — much less any dispensation flowing from it — must not be confused with love. We are strict with young people not because we do not care for them, but because we do. Such care summons up the imperatives of realism: discipline and, underlying this, obedience to wiser, older spirits. So far from constituting real love, sentimentality is consistent with cruelty and neglect. Indeed, these are just what it leads to.

Nor is a mildly policed classroom of highly motivated children an example of discipline abandoned. On the contrary, it means discipline so deeply internalised that minatory control has become effectively redundant. It is a gross error to think that this hidden order, this product of patient generations of work, can be easily universalised, effortlessly replicated among children coming from no such background of ingrained good habit.

The myth of self-esteem: false kindness is a form of cruelty

Sentimentality, like envy and pride, which it closely resembles, consists in indulging the self through the wilful pursuit of error. The educational version has both connived at idleness and insubstantiality, and identified false ills alleged to beset certain learners. Confusion rules, and since envy and pride are so contradictory, inevitably their incursions into a complex field like intellectual endeavour have left it even more confusing than it naturally is. The truth that some people are not very clever is not one sentimentalists will face at all, directly. One suspects that behind the denials and rationalisations, they actually see weak intellect as profoundly sinful on the part of the person in question, something to be covered up precisely by outraged evasiveness, which phrase stands in as another rough definition of extreme sentimentality.

It is most unreasonable to see low ability in this angry and intolerant light. On the contrary, it belongs to divine providence or blind chance. Whatever its provenance, it must be faced with fearless clarity and unremitting commitment. Instead, the sentimentalist summons up further evasive explanations to define an offensive reality out of court. Everybody is bright provided enough money is spent and all traces of competition and intellectual differentiation are banished. Everyone, lazy or not, must feel good. We may, of course, agree with the sentimentalist that the world hurts. Maybe it is bad news that talent is unequally distributed. Are we supposed to pretend we can outperform God or chance if only the soft abstractions are laced with sufficient saccharine and backed up with ever larger sums of taxpayers' money? Deep down the sentimentalist is one with the Utopian Marxist. They must both know it just is not so. There is a terrible rage locked up somewhere in all that mushy protestation.

As so often, reality is the kinder course. It is not shameful not to be clever. It is a poor show to take it lying down, though. Worse still is to be told to by those who affect to care about you. Sentimentality lets people deceive others as complacently as they fool themselves. Why is it so appealing? Because of the profligacy with which it generates error, and, when error is resisted and repudiated, because of the maudlin generosity with which it spawns further meretricious counter-arguments and measures.

Sentimentalists are indifferent to evidence. This holds *a fortiori* in the educational case. There is a vast evidence that progressivism has failed. The illiteracy, innumeracy and moral inadequacy of millions of people in America and Great Britain are unbudgeable facts. Progressives combine a fanatical devotion to abstractions on the one hand with a preternatural indifference to such facts on the other.

The nonsense of self-esteem

As truth keeps peering or glaring through the fog of dishonesty, further supplementary devices and conceits are evolved to reduce its force. Hence the popularity of the concept 'self-esteem', paradoxically promoted by an ethos which also denigrates effort. If you do not work hard at school, why should you feel great self-esteem? Yet as idle as you may be, self-esteem is reckoned your due portion.

The rearing of children, their moral and cognitive formation, is an exacting task needing exceptional clarity of insight and unbending determination to act in their interest. Instead, all too often in America and Britain, we let undisciplined feelings cloud our better judgement. This warps thinking. Because adults love their children, there is a temptation for us to romanticise the adult/child relationship in all its contexts, to get tearful and cloying about what being a child means, even to the extent of wanting to isolate childhood from the pains of the general human condition. Thus flourishes the error that the springtime of life — childhood and adolescence — can and should somehow be removed from the heartache, pain and hard choices of the world. While the ideology of childhood is cloaked in a language of 'helping children', 'recognising individual differences', and 'building pupil self-esteem', the net effect is instead to soften standards and get everyone off the hook. This does no one any favours. It is actually a cruelty to blight people's lives by colluding in their ignorance.

False pity means teachers do not demand too much of students. If the work is difficult it makes them feel bad about themselves; fewer tests are easier for all concerned; highly relativistic standards mean that no one is stretched, no one fails, no one points a finger, no one feels badly about his or her efforts, and no one is identified as a winner or loser. In the United States the result is that students graduate from school with high 'self-esteem' but weak skills and relatively little knowledge. We can usefully compare this to Japanese students who feel nervous about what they know and do not know but, in fact, have performed far higher on all tests.[20]

Self-esteem will not last long for high school 'graduates' who cannot read, write, compute or understand geography, history or sciences: they find few good jobs and are cut off from many avenues of continuing and higher education.

In Britain we see the same neglect posing as concern. The facts of the world, like the brutal truth that there is now little demand for unskilled labour, so that it is absurd on practical grounds, aside from the wrong done to children, to allow people to finish secondary school in a state of ignorance, are sentimentally resented and ignored. The abstractions about childhood's need for personal space and children's 'right' to their own 'culture' are sugary cover for the wickedness of the progressive credo. Other people pay and suffer. So that the progressive soul shall glow inwardly, the weak are locked for ever into that weakness, the likelihood being that they will form part of a cycle of hopelessness and dependency.

There is also a penumbra of ignorance which surrounds actual illiteracy and other deficits. There are millions who can read, but not properly. The same holds across the curriculum. There are millions of young people who get to their late teens only to realise that after years of being told to feel good about themselves, they have little chance of entering the professions, or even of securing a decent, self-fulfilling life for themselves.

Institutional sentimentality in educational administration

Nor is the sentimentality of education confined to the classroom, though such a confinement would just in itself be a civilisational disaster. On the contrary, the corrupting deceit operates also on the administrative and policy level. The entire school enterprise in the United States has been deluged with sentimental claims about the specialness of 'public education' as the only legitimate vehicle for learning and social mobility. Other forms of education, particularly private and parochial schools, are seen as antipatriotic, divisive, and against the best interests of children and society.

Things are much the same in Britain. Any attempt, for example, to challenge the hegemony of the neighbourhood comprehensive school is met with cries of hatred and condemnation. Sentimentality — indifference to evidence and love of abstract equality — is here intermeshed with envy and guilt. The introduction by the last Conservative Government of schemes to allow greater freedom to headteachers from politicised local authorities, and still more the public funds allowing clever, disadvantaged children to go to expensive private schools, have generated the most appalling hatred. The latter policy has been revoked by the new Labour Government as a sop to its backbenchers.

As for private schooling, in the ranks of the education elite, it is plain anathema. It is strange that those who would see nothing bad in fellow citizens having expensive holidays in the Caribbean, or buying luxurious houses, should get so hot and bothered about people spending their money making sure their children are properly taught. The response to the failure of the state schools is equally remiss. Rarely are they blamed for their lack of purpose, of order, of sound values. Instead a wilful refusal to accept evidence is witnessed in sentimental excuses. The state schools must take everyone; the private schools, or the British opted-out schools, can cream off the ablest boys and girls through careful screening. They can expel trouble-makers. They can demand higher standards.

Here is another sentimental trick: the citing of what is true, in a bad cause, the use of what considered clearly can sustain far better construction than the sentimental case puts on it. These charges really mean some schools are superior. This is why people are prepared to pay through the nose for their children to attend them. This is why they search them out, or move house to be near good state schools, sometimes as a substitute for paying privately. Many people in America and Britain are prepared to make such sacrifices for those they love most of all: their children.

Nor does it dawn on these dogs-in-the-manger that if it were seriously proposed we be denied free choice in supermarkets or housing or the purchase of cars, they would be as outraged as anyone else. It is grossly sentimental to make exceptions, absent a highly developed intellectual and moral case. School has been wrapped in a sentimental cocoon, whose effect has been to spare it the exposure to those forces of competition whereby economies prosper. Worse, it has even been spared proper economic analysis.

Sentimentality promotes failure

By definition, sentimentalists do not recognise the sad results of their sentimentality. They maintain that their mission is to take all comers, but more than this, to accept children as they are, to avoid judgmental reckoning of their cultural and educational performance, to establish in them all a sense of worth. Humbug! There are millions of men and women in good positions in America and Britain who were born in very humble circumstances. They got on, however, because their schools did indeed take all comers, and then push them as far as possible. If they were clever, their teachers were rightly more concerned with their academic worth than with any fictive self-worth. They were expected to flourish academically, not left to so-called working-class values — a quietist-style insult to good working-class parents who want their children to do well.

The syrupy mix of relativist standards, expectations and assessments has been glossed with the phrase 'equality of opportunity'. This is the most dishonest and sloppy phrase at present operating in American and British education. In truth you cannot achieve equality of educational opportunity until you make all homes equally rich, clever and encouraging. In other words, you never can.

What you can do, for some people, as the old Communist tyrannies used to do for most, is force down standards: equality of output, not opportunity. For a distressingly large minority of the American and British populations exactly such a downward convergence of performance has been achieved. The huge tail of underachievement in American and British schools represents a kind of grotesque Sovietisation in miniature, supported by comparably grotesque sentimental apologetics.[21]

Financial sentimentality

It is strange, given the absence of a real socialist tradition in America, that the socialist educational straitjacket is in some ways more constricting there than in Britain. America's marvellous parochial schools, for example, are utterly denied public funding, an anomaly exceeding anything on the British scene. But in Britain too, there is fanatical resistance to economic rationality. There is hostility to private education, and to any financial measures which might narrow the distance between the private sector and the much less successful state sector. And the pro-state school case is put in both countries as if parents of private pupils paid no taxes, and contributed nothing to society. By a surpassing injustice, they are deemed entitled to have their children attend non-state schools — if indeed at all — only if they pay the whole bill.

This segmentation of finance into 'public' and 'private' is a very sentimental conceit. It has emotional force, but no grounding in economic reason. 'Our money' is somehow sanctified by its going in the form of tax revenues to the state schools; 'their money' is somehow sullied by its being privately controlled. It is notable that in Britain, even during the 18 years of Conservative administration between 1979 and 1997, the Government was quite unable to get a voucher plan operating. This was despite the long and sophisticated advocacy of Arthur Seldon at the Institute of Economic Affairs.[22]

Sentimentality over standards and testing

The elite in America and Britain are expert at dissembling on the question of standards. They shift about in a way wholly consistent with our view that their attachment is emotional rather than rational. Standards have not fallen, or examination results do not matter, or there is more to school than learning dead facts, or low standards could be put right by government funds — all these shifting, often mutually contradictory answers are returned to the conservative critic indelicate enough to mention the shocking cognitive deficits in our two countries.

If the whole population really knew what sentimental hypocrisy was in charge of the schools their children attend, there would be a rebellion. The aim of high achievement for our children is looked on with horror by the elite as a middle-class imposition. This posture combines the self-fixation of the modern intelligentsia with its equally false self-criticism, the latter nothing more than vanity in thin disguise. In America, William Glasser, writing very much in the spirit of that supreme sentimentalist and destroyer of schools, Carl Rogers, identified in one of his titles, *Schools without failure*, just what the sentimental model of a good school is. It is one which does not make children feel bad by pointing out where they have fallen short of some externally validated standard.[23]

Thus far we have sounded pessimistic. This need not be the case, since there are some grounds for thinking that sentimental education has had its great days. There are sounds and stirrings of a realistic fightback, and it is to these we now turn.

Has sentimentality a school future?

In 1992, the US Congress actually authorised and funded the National Council on Education Standards and Testing, a group established to investigate a possible national system of assessment. Immediately, certain Congressional Leaders, mainly Democrats, on the House Education and Labor Committee, appeared to balk at the next, logical step, establishing national standards and then testing students to see if they are meeting them.

The resistance was vociferous. On January 29, 1992, a *New York Times* headline announced: 'Prominent educators oppose national tests'.[24] Fifty well-known educators and testing experts publicly criticised a proposal by the bipartisan National Council on Education Standards and Testing to establish a national curriculum and national tests: 'A national examination — even elegantly realised in regional variations and alternative formats — may well drive schools toward mindless accountability'.[25] The choice of words is revealing. Is mindless (or wilful) *unaccountability* supposed to be better? Moreover, even if, as some scholars think, the idea of a centralised curriculum is unviable, the thing to note in the response of one of the more prominent of our 50 good people and true, is its perverse and reflex hostility to accountability in the use of public funds.

The Council's proposal, it seems, flies in the face of a revered American tradition: letting states and local authorities determine school goals, curriculum and examinations. 'This would be a radical departure', Susan Chira of *The New York Times* explained, 'from the long standing American tradition of local control of curriculums that has led to a patchwork of uneven course requirements, tests and school results.'[26] Reactions to the belated effort to institute national standards and testing in the United States illustrate the difficulties. Since Britain has similar problems, and is further along, Americans can learn much about what may lie ahead in the United States as it tries to raise standards.

The example of Texas
A second example illustrates both struggle and stalemate in America. In Texas, the 1984 school reform law, based on a commission headed by Ross Perot, required all seniors to pass a mathematics proficiency test. In 1992, however, 8,000 students, mostly black and Latino, failed the test repeatedly. The State Board of Education lowered the passing grade from 60 to 55, permitting a further 1,763 students to graduate high school with their class. The public was outraged, though Texas Governor, Ann Williams, sent the students a note, which in sum let them off the hook.

The battle continued and the State Board reversed its decision, requiring the students to study for the examination again and re-take it. In a state where 40 per cent of children do not graduate high school, the pressure to raise standards, and then to lower them when students fail, seems likely to continue.[27]

The American failure to improve — and test — standards suggests a more powerful entrenchment by sentimental reaction than in Britain. This is not to endorse the bureaucratic centralism of the new British National Curriculum. Reborn competition promoted by the combination of national tests and *decentralising* education reform in

Britain in recent years — schools opting out of local authority control, managing their own finance, competing for the best pupils — is a far better reform tool than centralisation. The difference between the two countries does suggest, however, that reform initiative is less paralysed in the British case. Unless American reformers and those who resist them can work out some meaningful compromise, the see-sawing will continue both nationwide and at state level. American education, by the same token, will continue to flounder.

Sentimentality versus reason: the debate over standards

The opposing sides in educational controversy disagree about the nature of education and politics, indeed about the human condition. Disagreements are sharpest over the assessment of pupils. There is a conflict between *elite* and *democratic* approaches to standards. The American and British arguments are almost identical. In both countries, moreover, the controversy seems far from resolution. If the idea of sentimentality were brought into the discussion, the elite view would be seen to be clear and rational, the democratic view self-deceiving and sentimental.

Elitism has most unfairly been given a bad name. It is the honest pursuit of excellence, as Flew points out.[28] Elite standards divide students, sorting the brightest and most accomplished from the less able. Such standards are selective and exclusive, and their operation is sometimes painful in execution. The higher they are, the fewer those who can make them. We are talking about higher training, the best universities, the top jobs and the most opportunities. Elitists rejoice in their label, and believe competition between pupils is the only way to raise average standards.

The grade system has to be exactingly managed; those who cannot cope, fall away. In lots of ways the facts are sad. This is not an excuse for feeling sentimental about them. We need to identify and promote the best minds. We want the best possible leadership in science, mathematics, medicine, philosophy, industry, commerce and government. Any other outcome is unjust to the brilliant and industrious and to those who will benefit from their brilliance and endeavour. Justice and utility alike demand the highest and most rigorous testing. Anything else is cant.

The democratic claims are the opposite. All children need a fair and equitable education, which cannot happen if there is vicious intellectual competition. The children should all be in the same kind of institution, doing, effectively, the same sort of curriculum. Every child should be seen as a special person. All pupils should be encouraged to feel good about themselves.

Some democratic opinion thinks there should be no standardised testing at all. Such tests penalise, often very painfully, children from poor or bad homes and those who go to bad schools. The argument, persuasive perhaps at first blush, is that the state supplies these poor schools, tests and humiliates the children who unsurprisingly fail, and then blames them for their poor performance. It then escalates the testing, setting up an effective division between good schools and bad ones, and bright pupils and less successful ones.

This 'democratic' view — usually called 'progressive' in Britain — is very influential in both countries. In recent years the American and British educational establishments have fought every move by governments to lift standards, and they have done so precisely in this spirit.

The democratic case is that every person has merit and that democracies cannot long survive which systematically fail millions of their children. A huge, uncertificated underclass will lead to a divisive society with a weakened social fabric. The democratic refrain is for equal opportunities, getting everybody up to a satisfactory level.

This last argument can in part be returned in elitist form. Ignorance does threaten consensual politics and does create social fragmentation. The idea that all people have educational merit, on the other hand, is about as vacuous as the idea that they are all good at football or singing.

Sentimentality both panders to and expresses envy and guilt. The progressives feel (sic) that since not everyone can excel, then effectively no one should. No one should get results so shining that others might feel bad in comparison. This envy/guilt compound motors all socialist politics. The question we cannot answer is why such sentimentality targets education and not industry or commerce. Nor can we explain why people should tolerate it, now that it is dead in most other contexts, at the heart of the most important part of any modern economy — its education system.

Sentimentality may appeal to the envy of some whose children are not bright, though we doubt if most Americans and Britons are really so mean they cannot see that the general good requires a severe academic regime. The problem is the so-called intellectuals. Why should people themselves well educated, also fall into the trap? What they do is substitute the comforting warmth of their own tenderness for proper consideration either of children's development and life-prospects, or of the inexorably competitive nature of intellectual life, when it is authentically conducted.

Elite standards

Elite standards are concerned with whether students can master examinations held to reflect the traditional corpus of Western knowledge in its English (ie, American and British) form. The standard is the impersonal one of a great tradition. It corresponds directly to the performance of an elite minority of schools. Elitism means public standards privately achieved. Democracy in standards means private individuality — whatever talents each individual can be found to possess on careful search thereof — publicly celebrated. The search in the latter case is for something at which every child can excel. It is hard, frankly, to see this as having any real meaning in educational terms.

It is far easier to achieve high standards if you have a largish minority of students at elite institutions. Such students supply a model of excellence. The whole testing system can base itself, in progressively thinned-down form, on their performance. Once you have a common institution like the regular American high school, especially when it operates under an egalitarian ideology, it becomes very hard to maintain a high academic standard.

The cost and logistic implications are different too. The elitist system requires the expensive grading of individual written work of a high intellectual quality. Democratic systems permit and require a mass machine-graded, norm-referenced test system, around work of a low intellectual quality.

Progressive standards are personal and relative, decrying the 'objectivity' of the elitists with their harsh screening. In both countries, progressives oppose streaming students by ability. In practice, though, the systems work differently. The major way into a British university is to take the 'A' level examination (Advanced Level of the General Certificate of Education). This is available *de facto* only to a minority of students. It is embarked on in the main by students of 16 years of age or older. Candidature is normally governed by prior performance. There are now alternative ways (mostly rather easier) to get to university; but 'A' level remains the standard route. There is no British equivalent of the Scholastic Aptitude Test, a 'democratic' measurement, designed expressly to be curriculum and syllabus-free, indeed, in principle not even related to what children are taught at school. In this regard, American education remains more sentimental and ineffective than British.

Sentimentality in pedagogy and curriculum

Sentimentality influences teaching and the curriculum. Both in America and Britain, practices are often mushy to the point of pabulum. Tests are out, portfolios (projects and continuous assessment) in. Instruction is replaced by 'group work', 'exploration' and self-defined learning. In America, curriculum error remains more obstinate than in Britain. In (American) English lessons, phonics, grammar, syntax, parsing, vocabulary, essays and editing are largely lost arts. In the British case, some of these are coming back. In the USA, mathematics is all but lost in 'word problems' and the use of hand calculators to replace the ability to add, subtract, multiply and divide. Again, the return to sanity has begun earlier in Britain.

In both countries, however, history is sacrificed on the altar of relevance. 'Knowing your community' is more important than the origins of modern Europe. Multicultural, multilingual and, frankly, mere 'pop' literature replace the classics. There is often an interest in the literature of cultures which had no writing until modern times.

The worst practical scandal, noted by Sizer in America, but true also of Britain, is the compact between teachers and pupils to go easy on each other.[29] Perhaps worst of all on the intellectual level is the mixing of sentimentality with a reductionist materialism. It is widely believed that the key variable in successful learning is financial resource input, and that the only good classes are small classes. These sentimental myths are worse than wrong, since they positively inspire wrong models of human achievement. It would be a good sign if just one leading American or British politician dared to challenge this sentimental orthodoxy. It is, after all, hard to combat unidentified pathologies.

Getting on with it: the end of 'feel good' education

The easy appeal of sentimentality in education is also its greatest weakness. Vapid at best, shallow and venal at its worst, this go-easy, soft and overly romanticised view cannot prevail as a guiding principle in modern education, or not for long. As this chapter has shown, sentimentality demeans students, treating them in a soppy, romanticised way on the one hand, and in a paternalistic, pitying fashion on the other. This view of children and their capacities begins with a compromise verging on a conspiracy. It is easier somehow to feel sorry for youth than to hold them accountable at the highest standard and then to push them to reach it. And this go-light approach (compromise) gets the teacher off the hook as well: after all 'these kids can't really learn much anyway, so why not let them enjoy their school years?'

Already, in Great Britain and the United States, we see four trends that spell the end of 'feel-good' as the basis for schooling. First, *better information* on student and school performance is exposing the results of squandering education on the sentimental perspective. Secondly, *active school markets* mean that families can 'opt out' of ineffective schools, thus granting parents and students more choice and submitting educators to greater inter-school competition. Thirdly, *rising standards* imposed by governments at all levels expose sentimentalism for what it is, and beg for stiffer requirements and harsher evaluations (tests). And, fourthly, *alternative access to knowledge through technology* means that parents can break the hegemony of the state system and through television, videos, the Internet and other computer technology, can access education directly for their children. These trends — better knowledge of student achievement, stronger market forces, higher and more measurable standards, and new technological avenues for gaining knowledge and skills — taken together hold great promise in the near future.

More accountability threatens sentimentality

Both the US and UK (England and Wales) are witnessing greater freedom of and increased accessibility to better information on school methods and student attainment. Citizens in all capacities (eg, parents, taxpayers, voters, business leaders) are witnessing the disastrous results of coddling students, and they are appalled. What was once a closed system of information has now become more public, available, and open. Unavailability and obscurity have been replaced with publicity and praxis.

A case in New York State is informative. Since the arrival of the new New York state commissioner of education, Dr Richard Mills, in 1995, a grade-specific examination has been used, one based on *actual grade-level achievement*, not on 'minimum competency' in basic skills that sets a low standard. The target of testing has also changed: since minimum competency tests were aimed primarily at low-income and inner-city students (middle-class schools were hardly worried since most of their students met the minimums), the power of the information has also been changed. Now, suddenly, 99 per cent of middle-class students were no longer (as before) passing a minimum competency test (normed to detect students operating a grade level or more *below* the norm).

Parents in upper-class New York communities such as Scarsdale and Irvington in Westchester County, and Oyster Bay on Long Island, found suddenly that 30 to 40 per cent of their third grade (ages nine and ten) children were *not*, in fact, reading on the third grade level. These data on specific schools and districts (local education authorities) sounded an alarm bell in the well-to-do suburbs where family self-esteem and real housing values are geared to high test results and prestigious university admissions. Realtors immediately lost house sales. Parents went into orbit.

And superintendents (chief education officers) were forced to convene public meetings to try to explain the realities of the sub-standard achievement of students. School boards began to re-examine past practices: Scarsdale, NY, for example, had a policy of 'no homework until the fourth grade' based on some romanticised view that younger children might hurt themselves having to work extra on their lessons at home on their own. Teachers had blithely used so-called 'whole language' approaches to the instruction of reading and writing — which encouraged creativity but did not always instil accuracy in spelling, grammar and other testable standards. And parents wondered where their local tax money was going if between 30 and 40 per cent of their children were not performing to standard.

The state had a simple means for disseminating test results: they sent each newspaper, radio and television station in the state a disk with the performance of students in their region. The data just appeared in the local media — and schools were suddenly accountable and concerned about real information at each school level. The politics shifted from school boards, state agencies, and state and federal legislatures to each and every school and student. While conflict had not dissipated, it had focused: on learning, results, and the use of resources by schools.

Action followed knowledge. While school superintendents, defending their districts and jobs, tended to question the easy public access, the methodology, testing and sampling, the public read the results in the local paper and acted. Perhaps one method of loosening the stranglehold of bureaucracies over their data is to deliver the outcomes to the press and let the power of information take over. Certainly, as this case showed, school districts can move quickly to re-examine practice, use of funds and time, and policies on such things as assigning homework. Public opinion is more powerful than bureaucratic good intentions. Thus, parents are rejecting schools that flatter children but teach them little, a rejection based on better data and real results.

The power of choice and markets

Both nations have invested energy and resources in enhanced education choice since the 1980s: for example, magnet schools,[30] city technology colleges, charter schools,[31] grant maintained schools, open enrolment programmes, and even limited voucher schemes[32] to empower families to change schools. Markets are hardly sentimental: the 'invisible hand' of meeting parental demands with quality schooling is not easily romanticised, as schools are forced to compete, improve, and gain clients or close down.

It's the equivalent to Hayek's dismissal of *altruism* as a guiding force in national policy-making: like sentimentality in education, altruism may be appropriate in personal intercourse, such as within the family, church or synagogue, and other face-to-face settings, but it is usually a wrong concept in establishing health, welfare and foreign policies where feeling sorry for people leads to bad choices.

The effect of market competition is to weaken, if not to obliterate, sentimentality as parents move their children to a school that produces results, not excuses and soft, feel-good rationales for failure. Already, parents with adequate resources are seeking communities with stronger reputations for high test scores and records of obtaining places in good universities for their graduates. In Britain, education choices are more readily available than in the US since funds are spent on a far wider range of local and regional government schools, schools run by religious groups, and a host of new types of school: magnets, CTCs, opted-out schools, etc.

Unfortunately, the US is the only modern nation on earth that fails to subsidise its private and religious schools; thus parents either pay for tuition or suffer. Consequently, the parents of impoverished children who would most benefit, for example, from the disciplined, value-centred, God-fearing curriculum and climate of Roman Catholic schools (the largest system of private schools in the US) struggle to raise the money, despite the relatively low tuition (averaging only $1,600 annually for primary/elementary schools and $2,500 for Catholic secondary schools, compared to $14,000 per year in independent schools). For those who can afford these low tuition fees for Catholic education, the results have been encouraging: some of the poorest immigrant and other children of colour have responded to the regime of Catholic education and are achieving well above their state-school counterparts.[33]

These schools practise what one African American educator called 'tough love', a demanding but caring environment. As a black teacher put it: 'It's because I love you and care so much about your future success that I work you so hard — requiring lots of homework, and issuing you demerits when you under-perform or misbehave in school.' This is hardly a Rousseauian view of schooling, for children with the most to lose from a weak, unchallenging education.

Raising standards

In both nations, governments at all levels (in the US, federal, state and local) are embarking on the so-called 'standards movement' which *sets* a state (national) standard, *builds* a curriculum to meet that standard, and then, importantly, *tests* the students to ensure both that teachers have covered the material and that students have learned it. Test scores — when low — tend to blast sentimentality off the map and incite parents and other stakeholders to action.

Conservative Secretary of State for Education and Science, Kenneth Baker, insisted in 1987 that Britain adopt a national curriculum, standards, and tests. While implementation has been slow and painful — since writing a curriculum for 12 years around 11 'essential subjects' is no easy task — the results, by and large, have been positive: forcing educators to confront their students' successes and failures by providing 'league tables' on the front page of newspapers, showing just how well each school is performing. (Even the new Labour Prime Minister, Tony Blair, has no immediate plans, evidently, to dismantle the standards apparatus of British education.)

In the US, 40 states have recently raised 'the bar', requiring that schools and LEAs perform up to standard or risk being 'taken over' by the state. New Jersey now tests students in reading, writing and mathematics at grade levels 4, 8 and 12 (ages 10, 14 and 18) plus stipulating that in the 'off grades' (levels 1-3, 5-7 and 9-11) the school write and administer a similar test to help prepare students for the on-year tests. 'Performance indicators' are required in every subject: teachers must now show in writing just how they will know whether students are learning on target and on schedule — a far cry from the mushy, sentimental view that children should learn only what they want to, and when they wish.

New technology and access to knowledge

Finally, we see clear signs in the USA and UK that the technology revolution (the Information Age) is rapidly weakening the hegemony of formal (government-run) schooling, and affording parents and students access to the tools of learning directly. In particular, the Internet and other electronic networks put the world's knowledge literally at the fingertips of any eight-year-old able to 'sign on' and Surf the Web. Also, parents concerned about the lack of substance in government schools are 'buying' extra help directly from sources outside schools.

Hundreds of thousands of American students take cram courses to raise their scores on various required national tests, such as the Scholastic Aptitude Test (SAT) which is necessary for university admissions. Television advertising hawks learning packages and programmes such as 'Hooked on phonics', appealing to parents and even grandparents to overcome the apparent weaknesses of reading programmes based on such 'soft' concepts as Whole Language Instruction rather than basic phonics, grammar and spelling skills.

It will not be long before students worldwide will be linked together; where US and UK students studying French and French students learning English will log on and exchange ideas, materials and help over the Worldwide Web. Virtual schools may begin to replace weak and soft-headed 'real' schools, and teachers will be learners alongside their students or fall by the wayside.

Thus the future of sentimentality is by no means secure. It cannot and does not work: everyone knows that. Owning knowledge, skills, and abilities may 'feel good' in the end; but obtaining those states of grace (whether by studying, practising, repeating, drilling, and inquiring) is very hard work indeed, as every learned and skilled person knows. Ask a physician, priest, attorney, certified accountant, teacher, engineer, rabbi or airline pilot. Education, therefore, has the dual responsibility not only to convey the need for knowledge and skill, but also to give students the opportunities to obtain those personal habits of mind, virtues, fortitude, and manners so essential to success in life into the twenty-first century.

5

Back to a simple and pure nature

sentimentality and the environmental movement

Jo Kwong

Apocalyptic environmentalism is irrational
In a few short decades, the modern environmental movement has grown from a general interest in promoting broad environmental goals, such as improving air and water quality, to its current preoccupation of ridding the world of all pollutants and achieving 'zero risks' for society. Notably absent from these current endeavours is any reliance on or leanings towards rationality. Environmentalism has produced some of the most senseless, inane policies and outcomes imaginable.

In the name of the environment, the regulatory state has grown enormously, arguably to bestow a cleaner, healthier world to 'future generations'. Upwards of $30 million is spent in the US to 'save' habitat for the spotted owl. The price tag to roll carbon dioxide emissions back to 1990 levels is in the order of $7 trillion.[1] It costs over $600 million dollars to avert one death under certain water standards. Environmental advocates have waged war on chlorine, chloroflurocarbons, pesticides and other household chemicals at great cost to both manufacturers and consumers. Typical justifications for such expenditures claim that 'the environment is too special to place a price tag on', or 'we must protect the environment, whatever the cost'.

Environmentalism, as such logic suggests, is guided by a 'feel good' mentality — a mentality that exceeds common notions of sensibility. To illustrate, consider the following examples. While they may appear to be extreme, outrageous stories, in reality they represent rather straightforward synopses of our modern environmental being.

From The Cuyahoga River to dirt-eating rules
In 1969, a fire broke out on the waters of the Cuyahoga River in Ohio.

The imagery of the polluted waters lifted the infant environmental movement from its fringe beginnings and set it in the centre of a new awareness, focusing attention on the quality of the world's air, land, and water. In the US, sweeping seminal acts, such as the Clean Water Act and Clean Air Act were promulgated to demonstrate the new-found commitment to righting these wrongs.

In the decades since, lofty strides have been made. Water pollution levels decreased with total emission levels dropping 33.8 per cent between 1970 and 1990. Over the same period, lead levels in the air fell 96.5 per cent, and carbon monoxide levels in the air dropped 40.7 per cent.[2] These improvements, however, have not been sufficient to pacify environmental advocates. Instead, expectations have soared and a new class of nonsensical 'dirt-eating' guidelines currently rule — so named after the US Environmental Protection Agency directed that hazardous waste sites be restored to the level that a child could eat half a teaspoon of dirt every month for 76 years and not get cancer. Over half of the EPA's budget for hazardous waste clean-ups are spent complying with such rules, leading to the ridiculous instance, for example, in which water running off a cleaned-up site was required to be clean enough to drink without further treatment. Similarly, when soil tests on an 81-acre industrial site revealed that two ounces of 'hazardous' chemicals were mixed per ton of soil, the landowner was required to dig up more than 12,500 tons of soil and haul it — all 450 dump truck loads at a cost of $7,500 each — to a commercial dump in another state. EPA officials said they wanted to make the site safe enough to be used for *any* purpose.

From charismatic megafauna to self defence
The protection of biodiversity is a popular rallying cry for the modern environmental movement. The extinction of plant and animal species, it is argued, spells disaster for the planet. Consequently, a sophisticated federal system ensures that the actions of human beings are sufficiently held in check to protect flora and fauna. Endangered species legislation, like dirt-eating rules, have pushed environmentalism beyond common sense. Consider the case of Montana rancher John Shuler. Days after several of his sheep were killed by wildlife, he heard some commotion amongst his flock. He subsequently found three grizzly bears attacking his sheep and fired a few warning shots to frighten them away. But when Shuler noticed another large grizzly bear rearing up on his hind

legs, he did what most people would do in a heartbeat: he shot the bear. Environmental activists were 'up in arms' over the killing of an endangered species. Despite the fact that the Endangered Species Act makes exemptions for self defence, the Administrative Law Judge ruled that the self-defence plea did not apply since the rancher 'purposely placed himself in the zone of imminent danger of a bear attack'. The EPA fined Mr Shuler $4,000.

From 'everything is related to everything else' to wetlands

On the basis of the environmental mantra that 'everything is related to everything else', wetlands have achieved divine status among American environmentalists. Wetlands, better known as 'swamps' in pre-modern-environmental times, are hailed for their cleansing ability in the water cycle. The crusade to protect every piece of land that gets wet (even if it is 12 inches below the surface and only seven days out of a year — the going rule with the US EPA) has given rise to a litany of laughable stories. Most famous, perhaps, is the story of John Pozsgai, an immigrant from Hungary who cleared a parcel of land that had previously housed over 7,000 abandoned tyres. Instead of applauding his efforts, the government tossed Mr Pozsgai in jail for two years. Unbeknownst to him, the land was a 'wetland' and he had altered its use without the proper permits. In addition to the jail sentence, Mr Pozsgai was fined $200,000.

Two 70-year-old ranchers also unknowingly tested the wetlands waters. After a government water project flooded their Colorado land, the ranchers restored the river to its decades-old channel. The US Environmental Protection Agency subsequently sued, contending that when the river flooded the land it created an artificial 'wetland' that could not be dewatered without a permit.[3] Each rancher was fined $45 million.

While 'dirt-eating' rules govern hazardous waste clean ups, 'reasonable bird' rules evolved to deal with wetlands. In 1985, mid-western housing developer Hoffman Homes, complied with local authorities and filled in a shallow on-site depression where rainwater occasionally collected. Federal officials, however, fined Mr Homes for violating Clean Water Act rules originally intended to prevent people from filling and blocking riverways used by interstate commerce. When Mr Homes asked what interstate commerce he affected, the answer somehow pertained to birds. Migratory birds, you see, might visit the puddle and as they visited other puddles in other states, the birds became part of interstate commerce. Through a convoluted chain of political events, orders went out to EPA field offices advising them to claim jurisdiction over a 'wetland' if it could be used by migratory birds. The good news, at least in this case, is that a court of appeals overturned the EPA's $50,000 fine on Mr Homes and limited the 'reasonable bird' rule.[4]

Sense and sentimentality

The modern environmental movement is a crusade lacking both reason and common sense. Through effective imagery and packaging, environmental advocates have succeeded in securing policies and regulations, based not on analytical analysis, but on emotional and moral appeal. The outcomes of the acts, regardless of how irrational, ineffective, or downright stupid, are supported, defended, and expanded by creative twists on this old appeal.

Despite the 'warm and fuzzy' feeling that people are searching for through environmentalism, all is not warm and fuzzy. As the net of environmentalism is cast broader and broader throughout society — on developers, farmers, ranchers, and other everyday people — the impacts of the emotional decisions are growing and multiplying. As environmental advocates clamour for environmental protection at 'whatever the cost', its opponents are rising. Yet, the challenge is a difficult one. After all, who can argue against Mother Nature?

Sentimentality identifies the environment as 'a problem'

Prominent opinion leaders have embraced an environmental perspective that is premised upon a number of highly questionable assumptions. Assumptions which, for example, view the natural environment as benign and the manmade environment as harmful, which see corporations as evil agents and consumers as manipulated puppets, which see technological growth as anathema to environmental protection, or which hold that governments must be the ultimate protectors of the environment against destructive humans.

These types of assumptions, and the policies built upon them, have proliferated in the chaotic, disjointed arena of modern environmentalism. Certainly in the United States, and increasingly around the world, environmentalism has become a way of life touching virtually every choice and decision. Laws and regulations govern every natural and environmental resource imaginable: clean air acts, clean water acts, endangered species acts, forest planning acts, land use acts, hazardous wastes acts, to name a few.

From these acts emanate tighter and tighter regulations of chemicals used in widespread applications such as chlorine in water, ethanol in gasoline, and solvents in dry cleaning processes. Other laws govern more environmentally-remote aspects of daily living: the banning of air conditioners from new cars, because they are believed to impact the atmospheric ozone layer; the banning of polystyrene because it is thought to pose a solid waste problem; and the banning of aseptic juice boxes because they are difficult to recycle (despite their enormous efficiencies with regard to energy savings via refrigeration and ease of transportation).

Sentimentality is environmentally destructive

Growing numbers of cities require people to sort glass, aluminium and paper from their trash for expensive, inefficient recycling programmes. New laws mandate recycled content for manufacturing processes. Several states in the western US mandate the incorporation of recycled content into some plastic products. Some also specify recycled content requirements for glass containers, require use of recycled content in newsprint, and specify that a package must be reusable, source-reduced by 10 per cent, recycled at a 25 per cent rate, or must contain 25 per cent post-consumer content. These actions would be acceptable if reasonable recycling mechanisms were in place. Unfortunately, most recycling processes consume more resources and release more pollutants than their non-recycling counterparts. A surprising amount of properly sorted recyclables end up in landfills anyway, amounting to a massive waste of human energy and derailed good intentions.

The resemblance of the modern environmental movement to failed central planning efforts in former communist and socialist countries is remarkable. More than half of the 50 US states debated laws during the 1980s that would make it a crime to use disposable diapers. California considered banning the use of pesticides associated with the slightest possibility of causing cancer in laboratory rats. Landowners across the nation are finding their rights to use land severely restricted by laws ranging from wetlands to endangered species acts to global warming. And environmental advocates are seeking a total ban on that most useful of all chemicals, chlorine.

In public opinion polls, the American people reportedly support stricter government regulations to address concerns about environmental degradation. There is a prevailing misconception that we can simply legislate away serious environmental problems by passing tougher laws and ordering people to comply. There are, however, limits to the effectiveness of governmental regulatory controls particularly when they challenge good sense. Consider the following ridiculous example as told by Professor Thomas Di Lorenzo of Loyola University.

In 1991, the US Congress ruled that all sewage treatment plants had to remove at least 30 per cent of the organic waste from incoming sewage. This across-the-board inflexibility is obviously costly, but particularly so for cities which have very little organic matter in the first place. The sewage inflow of Anchorage, Alaska, for example, is typically cleaner than the federal government's prescribed levels of outflow. Nonetheless, the government held the city to its 30 per cent standard. Facing a $135 million dollar bill for a new sewage treatment plant that met the standard, the city alternatively opted for a cheaper, innovative solution: it invited two local fish-processing plants to dump 5,000 pounds of fish wastes into the sewer system. By subsequently removing the wastes, the city met its 30 per cent clean up limit. Surely, the impact on both the environment and the city's budget were not as intended, but they serve as an example of how the environmental 'feel good' mentality has run amuck.

Irrational policy, bolstered by sentimental visions of living in perfect harmony with nature, perpetuate the mind set that 'doing something' is preferable to doing nothing, even if the chosen actions are a complete failure in terms of environmental outcomes. Beyond the environmental failures, however, it is necessary to consider the broader consequences of the blind pursuit of environmental perfection.

The US Government's Council of Economic Advisors observes that regardless of one's view of the value of environmental improvement, the EPA's rigid regulatory strategy has clearly wasted a substantial portion of the nation's investment aimed at improving air quality — the cost of air pollution control during the 1980s has averaged more than $30 billion annually, and economic studies indicate that more cost-effective pollution control strategies could have achieved the same degree of environmental quality for billions less.

Robert Crandall at the Brookings Institution notes

The cost of environmental policy has been rising steadily and draining valuable resources from other productive uses. Much of this cost is unnecessary — the result of poorly designed legislation.[5]

Even Friends of the Earth, an international environmental advocacy group, has joined the chorus in attacking failed environmental pursuits. Its projects include a detailed list of federal spending that is blatantly anti-environmental.

The standard response to such critical assessments has been demands for greater government funding, stricter regulations, accelerated timetables for the phasing out of alleged pollutants, or simply, entirely new laws. Totally absent has been a calling for a renewed assessment of our environmental mindset. And so we find ourselves in a vicious Catch-22 which at times, appears utterly inescapable.

Sentimental environmentalism: a paranoid vision
Escaping from the Catch-22 requires a hard look at the feelings and emotions propelling the environmental vision. With little exception, most environmental comments are brimming with 'factoids' — bits and pieces of information, which, upon constant repetition, take on a semblance of truth. Perhaps no better example exists than the case of global warming. The catastrophic scenarios have been repeated so many times for so many years that most people believe our polar ice caps will soon be melting. Consider, for example, some comments from Jonathan Porritt, founder of Britain's Green Party:

> ...Friends of the Earth has been engaged in a campaign to halt the use of chloroflurocarbons (CFCs) in aerosols, sprays, and other processes. CFCs are not only destroying the ozone layer and therefore threatening to cause a massive epidemic of cancer, they are also a large cause of the "greenhouse effect". CFCs are probably the most destructive chemicals used in our industrial economy.[6]

Little public understanding has changed since Porritt penned those words in the 1980s. This acceptance grows despite the persistent efforts of people like atmospheric scientist Dr S Fred Singer, who tirelessly points out,

> The ban on CFCs has been based more on scare tactics than on sound science. We have absolutely no observations and no evidence to show an increasing trend of ultraviolet radiation, and

certainly, no massive epidemic of skin cancer that can be related to CFCs.[7]

Yet those who attempt to calm or counter the environmental fear-mongering by looking at scientific evidence and analytic analysis are typically attacked as being 'anti-environmental'. Lost in the war of words is the basic realisation that most people prefer cleaner air to dirtier air, cleaner water to dirtier water, and pristine landscapes to polluted ones. What differs, of course, is their alternative perspectives about how to achieve environmental amenities. It may be the case, however, that cries of 'anti-environmentalist!' are far more effective in capturing the moral highground in the environmental wars against common sense.

Back to nature and down with technology: a sentimental fantasy

Underlying the sentimental vision is a perception that our high tech world has destroyed man's ability to have a 'oneness' with nature. Technology is viewed as a culprit and a return to a less hurried, less modern way of life offers an idyllic vision of 'earthkeeping'.

Writing for *The Progressive*, Murray Bookchin says,

Perhaps the most obvious of our problems is uncontrollable growth. In modern societies, *unlimited* economic growth is assumed to be evidence of human progress. Growth is, in fact, almost synonymous with the market economy that prevails today in the United States and the world. That fact finds its clearest expression in the popular business slogan, "Grow or die". We live in a competitive world in which rivalry is a law of economic life.[8]

Arguing that a market economic system is incompatible with a sustainable way of life, the socialist journal, *Monthly Review*, opined

It follows that what has to be done to resolve the environmental crisis, hence also to insure that humanity has a future, is to replace capitalism with a social order based on an economy devoted not to maximising private profit and accumulating ever more capital but rather to meeting real human needs and restoring the environment to a sustainable healthy condition.[9]

Putting it most succinctly, Jonathan Porritt writes, 'Simply put, our modern society is unsustainable.'[10]

Not only is modern society unsustainable, it is undesirable. The Sierra Club recently appealed for donations by 'reminiscing' about days long gone.

Our country looked quite different 104 years ago when the Sierra Club was founded. The Everglades *still* covered nearly the entire southern half of Florida and sustained a dazzling array of flora and fauna. The inspiring peaks of Yosemite and awesome rockscapes of the Grand Canyon could *still* be viewed through clear vistas. Humankind's relentless drive to "tame" nature was in full swing, but *vast unspoiled stretches of forest, prairie, and coastline still existed*...Neither you nor I had a chance to breathe that clean air or pause on a hike to cup our hands and drink from a mountain stream without concern that toxic chemicals had contaminated the headwaters...But we can try to imagine it...[11]

The flaw in this sentimentality, however, lies in the poor recollection these advocates have of times long gone. Tackling the folly of these sentiments head on, the late Dixy Lee Ray described the far more 'natural' world of her childhood in the early 1900's:

The world in which I spent my early years was a very smelly place. The prevailing odours were of horse manure, human sweat, and unwashed bodies. A daily shower was unknown; at most there was the Saturday night bath.

Indoors the air was generally musty and permeated by the sweetly acrid stench of kerosene lamps and coal fires. It was the era of the horse and buggy, the outhouse, and dirt. Depending upon the weather, it was either dusty or muddy.

As she goes on to further describe the conditions of her childhood, Ray points out two fields of remarkable progress — food production and medicine, pointing out that human life is no longer totally dependent upon the whims of uncaring nature and the availability of already existing natural resources. 'We have been privileged,' she wrote, 'to live through the most extraordinary five decades of expanding knowledge and its use for bettering life that the world has ever known. Little wonder that some people cannot cope.'[12]

At a recent environmental conference, two university professors shared similar thought experiments they had developed to help students sort out conflicting emotions on perspectives of the past. One asked his students, 'If you could spend $50,000 in a Sears Roebuck catalog, would you rather select from the 1900 catalogue or the 1997 catalog?' Consistently, over two-thirds of the students opted for the latter.

The second professor asked his students 'Would you trade places with the wealthiest person of the 1900s?' Again, there were few takers once the students considered the absence of long distance phone calls, air travel, microwaves, automatic teller machines, and the like. Similarly, I suspect environmental advocates also recognise the benefits of the modern world, but nonetheless hang onto a sentimental notion of the past, readily ignoring its vast drawbacks and inconveniences.

Not everything natural is good
Let's take another look at the environmentalist vision that all things manmade are somehow inferior to their 'natural' counterparts. Organic produce, for example, is touted as healthier than fruits and vegetables grown with manmade pesticides. Scientific evidence, however, suggests the organic produce is not all it's cracked up to be.

Leading cancer researcher Bruce Ames of the University of California points out that natural is not necessarily healthier. Plants survive by their own brand of chemical warfare. Lacking claws and teeth to protect themselves, plants produce toxic compounds that make them distasteful to predators. By breeding insect-resistant plants instead of using chemical pesticides, we encourage plants to raise their levels of these natural toxins. The end result is that organic produce often contains much higher levels of toxic, cancerous chemicals than fruits and vegetables grown with manmade pesticides.

Fortunately, humans are well protected against low doses of toxins by an internal defence system that fails to distinguish between synthetic and natural toxins. Humans, it turns out, are exposed to 10,000 times more natural carcinogens than manmade. In other words, fully 99.99 per cent of the potential carcinogens that we ingest are created naturally — but with little risk to us.

Ironically, environmental initiatives to ban certain pesticides end up causing more harm than good. As Ames's research indicates, we get far more benefit from eating fruits and vegetables than from avoiding them, despite popular perceptions about pesticides and chemicals. The more we do to make fresh produce readily available, the greater the health benefits. Policies which raise the cost of fruits and vegetables, such as pesticide bans, have the opposite effect.

Economic growth: not bad news for the environment

A corollary to the technology-is-bad-for-the-environment hypothesis is the belief that we must reverse or halt economic growth in order to stem the tide of environmental degradation. Opinion polls consistently suggest that people increasingly associate environmental degradation with economic growth. The assumption is that technological and industrial progress, along with economic growth, are creating some sort of industrial monster that has raged out of control. And with it come new forms of pollution and other environmental harms.

One need only look at the former Communist countries to see the fallacy in claiming that economic growth causes pollution. The International Union for Conservation of Nature and Natural Resources reported, for example, that 33 per cent of East German lakes, 95 per cent of Polish rivers, and 70 per cent of rivers in the former Czechoslovakia are 'dead or heavily polluted'. The Eastern European countries are among the most highly polluted areas of the world, even though the standard of living has been considerably lower than in its Western European counterparts. Similarly, the industrialised nations of Europe and North America have cleaner air and water and healthier populations than the less developed nations in Asia, Africa, and Latin America.

Ironically, economic growth is viewed as the enemy to the environment. In reality, economic growth offers one of the greatest hopes for environmental improvement in the developing world through its ability to lift people out of poverty. Poverty and environmental degradation necessarily go hand in hand. In the developing world, people often have no choice but to strip the forests bare to secure food and heat sources; they have little choice but to use waterways for bathing, cooking, and cleaning. Understandably, they have little interest in the modern environmental preoccupation of securing 95 per cent or 99 per cent clean water.

Increased prosperity resulting from economic growth boosts the demand for environmental improvement. As income levels and living standards rise, people increasingly focus on ways to enhance and improve their surroundings. Our ability to address global environmental improvements becomes more reasonable. These critical links, however, are generally lost upon environmental do-gooders. International environmental meetings, held in places such as Cairo or Beijing, typically focus not on giving the world's children access to water, but on the best ways to deny developing countries access to modern technology.

The ongoing global warming policy dilemma is another case in point. Proponents of global warming catastrophe fear the developing world will add more and more 'warming' gases to the atmosphere as their economies grow. Yet what right does any country have to deny these younger economies the opportunity to pull themselves out of poverty?

Corporations not enemies of the environment

Another driving force of the modern environmental vision is the conviction that the corporation is public enemy number one. Recall that a central justification for a strong federal presence in environmental protection stems from the belief that corporations will always do wrong by the environment. Specifically, people fear that the drive to earn high profits causes corporations to exploit environmental resources. Looking beyond the sentimental outbursts, we find, however, that the profit motive can actually work to the benefit of the environment.

Businesses need to make a profit in order to survive, so each company faces the incentive to consider carefully the prices of the natural and environmental resources that it uses. If a particular resource is in short supply, its price will be higher than others that are more readily available. It makes little sense for a producer to use, or 'waste', the higher priced resource unless there are no substitutes. Where no substitutes exist, the price incentive encourages the search and development of appropriate alternatives. The pursuit of profits, then, is actually a driving force to help conserve resources.

In the absence of prices for natural resources, however, this process cannot work. Unpriced goods, such as government-owned resources provided 'free' to all users, like public parks, are often poorly managed and used. When people don't pay the full cost of a resource, they have little incentive to use it carefully. The result can be traffic jams, litter, and damaged property. For this reason, it is important to allow markets to price goods, rather than governments. Doing so enables the profit motive to work in favour of conservation.

Most of the examples that come to mind when we talk about corporations exploiting the environment arise when common property is involved. Common property is that which is typically owned by a government for the 'common good' of the people. When hundreds, thousands, or millions of people jointly own a resource, like the air, the forests, or the oceans, no one person has the incentive to take care of it and to see that resources are managed carefully and responsibly.

Consider the problem of over-fishing of the oceans. Conventional environmental wisdom touts that most major species of commercially valuable marine life are being over-fished. The reason is that fishermen from different nations face stiff competition to be the first to get their catch. With publicly owned resources, this type of competition is to be expected.

Alternatively, secure property rights can eliminate the 'use it or lose it' mentality that governs common property. Economists have found, for example, that when fishermen leased privately owned oyster beds, they not only practised more conservation but also received higher profits than fishermen who fished in states where oyster beds are owned by the government. Similarly, with privately owned aquaculture operations (fish farms), stocks are carefully controlled and maintained in a way that is difficult, if not impossible, to do in open-access waters.

Animal rights pits the interests of animals against those of humans

With its talk of interconnectedness and interdependence, it's not surprising to see environmentalism's link to the animal rights movement. For instance, in the journal *Earth Ethics: evolving values for an Earth Community*, former chief executive officer of The Humane Society of the United States, John Hoyt writes

> Central to the emerging world ethic is the recognition that nature (including animals) has integrity and value independent of its utility to humans...When we say that animals have rights, we mean that, as a philosophical principle, animals should be included within the same system of moral protections that govern our behavior towards each other...In the philosophical sense, the rights of animals are derived not from legal statutes but from the same principles of justice and fairness that are the foundation of human rights.[13]

While balancing the interests of animals with those of humans indeed poses a challenge to animal lovers, there are others who seize on the animal rights movement to advance alternative agendas. The protection of endangered species, for example, is one way to 'look out' for the flora and fauna that otherwise are unable to express their desires to humans. Alternatively, the Endangered Species Act has been used to pit the interests of animals against those of humans. The sentimental, emotional, fact-less approach to environmentalism has left us wide open to such abuses. After all, absent a litmus test for rationality, where do we draw the line?

The northern spotted owl has become a classic example of man versus nature. It all started as a surrogate for yet another environmental pursuit: the protection of 'ancient' forests. Environmental advocates decided that old trees should be preserved, yet this spur of the moment pursuit lacked statutory backing. Recognising the shaky ground for legislative action, they decided to put the endangered species act to the test.

As Sierra Club Legal Defense spokesmen Andy Stall commented:

> Until legislation is adopted which protects these forests, we need at least one surrogate, if you will, that will provide protection for the forests...Well, the northern spotted owl is the wildlife species of choice to act as a surrogate for old-growth protection, and I've often thought that thank goodness the spotted owl evolved in the Northwest, for if it hadn't we'd have to genetically engineer it. It's a perfect species for use as a surrogate.[14]

The protection of the spotted owl rolled out of control. Never mind the thousands of timber-related jobs that were lost, the devastation to local economies, or the sheer financial loss to individuals and corporations that owned newly unharvestable land. Instead, the focus was on the uniqueness of the northern spotted owl and the implications of losing yet another species in the great web of life. There were, however, growing intellectual problems for the spotted owl protectors.

The northern spotted owl, some biologist pointed out, is not genetically distinct from other owls that live up and down the coastline of the western United States and Mexico. In 1990 when ornithologist George Barrowclough, of the American Museum of Natural History in New York, and biologist Ralph Gutierrez, of Humboldt State University in California, compared chromosome fragments from the northern and Californian spotted owls 'no genetic difference was found' between the two. They further noted no significant difference between DNA samples of northern and 'Mexican' spotted owls, which roost in the scrub desert of the Southwest and Mexico.[15]

Nor are their numbers as low as reported. Owl sightings varied tremendously, particularly given their nocturnal behaviour. Each time reports were generated about the dwindling number of remaining spotted owls, new populations would be 'discovered'. Additionally, biologists discovered that the owls will, in fact, nest in younger trees.

Their existence is not directly linked to old growth forests as the environmental advocates claim.

Cuteness — of owls — undermines rational perspectives

These scientific findings, however, were lost amidst the momentum of the issue. Cute photos of owls popped up on bumper stickers, book covers, magazine covers, and T-shirts. They became the symbol of human arrogance: in our quest for material and economic gain, the lives of these adorable creatures had become expendable. Until, of course, environmental advocates took note and launched the crusade.

The spotted owl controversy pitted more environmental advocates against 'common folks' than other issues of the day. Instead of revealing the human arrogance of mankind, people questioned the arrogance of the environmentalists. To this day, the battle lines are drawn, with the 'wise users' pitted against environmental and animal advocates.

Beyond such melodramas lies another contingent of animal rights activists. The People for the Ethical Treatment of Animals (PETA), for example, are opposed to using animals in scientific studies to save or improve human lives. 'Even painless research is fascism,' says Ingrid Newkirk, founder of PETA. 'Even if animal research resulted in a cure for AIDS, we'd be against it,' she adds. Her perspectives, perhaps are summed up by her simple words: 'A rat is a pig is a dog is a boy.'[16]

John Hoyt proposes a paradigm for rights of animals in which rights are determined by a balancing test for 'overriding values'. If we seek to balance the interests of animals with that of humans, we will often find that

> [the] animals' interests are clearly weightier but need to be asserted as independent, cognizable interests. For example, rabbits are used to test the eye-irritancy of new cosmetics. Yet, our interest in new eyeliners and facial creams is frivolous compared to the suffering test rabbits endure. Therefore, the animals' interest in not being subjected to unnecessary pain should outweigh the human interest in self-adornment.

The problem with Hoyt's balancing test is obvious. The middle-aged woman who is just starting to notice the effects of 'maturity' is likely to weigh the alternatives quite differently from the typical non-cosmetic oriented male.

Hoyt finds it insufficient to simply argue that as moral beings, *people* must respect and care for animals. 'When we speak of "being kind to animals" we are really talking about states of mind or motivations that are gratifying to human beings,' he writes. Alternatively, Hoyt sees the need to shift our focus away from human-oriented motivations and gratifications toward the intrinsic worth and needs of animals.

The dangers in this line of thought, however, are quite apparent. Writing for *The Freeman*, Robert James Bidinotto says

> Any intelligible theory of rights must presuppose entities capable of defining and respecting moral boundary lines. But animals are by nature incapable of this. And since they are unable to know, respect, or exercise rights, the principle of rights simply can't be applied to, or by, animals. Rights are, by their nature, based on a homocentric view of the world.

Economist P J Hill also argues that man must be the centre of our considerations:

> It may well be that trees have in some ultimate moral sense, rights. However, if those rights are to be protected by human institutions it will be because humans are the repository of those rights. Individuals can include the welfare or preferences of trees within their own set of preferences and thus grant those rights to the trees. But those rights will only exist because individuals have rights.

Giving rights to nature leads to the question 'Who will act as nature's representative?' The rights-to-nature approach will ultimately expand privileges to private environmental organisations which will clamour the loudest to act as the spokesmen. And as this litany has shown, the environmental movement needs no further legitimation to create new irrational policies.

Environmentalism is sentimentality at its worst
What explanation can be offered for these ludicrous manifestations of environmentalism? I propose that environmentalism has been the victim of sentimentality at its worst. Through the creation of an idyllic image for the world and how it *could* be if we eliminated every environmental 'bad', environmental advocates have successfully nurtured and refined an environmental mentality that risks common sense and rational analysis. Furthermore, through the broadened net of global environmentalism, in which 'everything is linked to everything else', the affects of the movement are perpetuated well beyond the

developed world and into the less fortunate world in which the daily struggle for food and shelter are foremost. What sense does it make to fight for 99 per cent pristine water when the world's poor lack access to water at all? What sense does it make to pursue regulations that devastate local economies and wealth generation, when in fact, poverty is the single biggest threat to environmentalism? It is these and other broad questions that come to mind when we consider what surely must be sentiment and emotion in propelling a movement that upon closer examination, has little grounding in reason and reality.

6

All feelings and no doctrine

the sentimentalisation of religion

Peter Mullen

Sentimentality brings about the end of doctrine

Imagine a room with the furniture removed so that nothing remains except the smell of escaping gas. This is a parable of sentimentality: for sentimentality is what is left when everything substantial has been taken away — form, content, order and reasonable purpose. It is the self-inflicted fate of the Church in the last third of the twentieth century.

The removal of form from the Church, the New Deformation, has been accomplished by two fashionable tendencies: the liberal theology of demythologising and the so called 'happy-clappy' revivalism of the Charismatic Movement. Traditional belief and practice have been trapped between these pressures and squeezed until they are all but suffocated.

Liberal theology: our image of God must go

Liberal theology has, of course, been a strong revisionary tendency since the mid-nineteenth century when first German professors such as Strauss and Bauer rejected the miracle stories of the New Testament and then, beginning with *Essays and Reviews* (1860), the fashion for demythologising took hold among theologians in the English-speaking world. The liberal tendency was largely ignored by the ordinary churchgoer who well into the twentieth century, remained content to attend Mattins or Evensong, or the increasingly popular Parish Communion — though not perhaps as frequently as he had done before the First World War. It was not until the 1960s and the coming of affordable mass-market paperback books on all serious subjects that the ideas of the liberal demythologisers — current in academic circles for more than a century — were noticed by the ordinary churchgoer.

The bombshell was the popular paperback *Honest to God* (1963) by J A T Robinson, advertised by a shock-horror article in *The Observer* entitled 'Our Image Of God Must Go': all the more shocking and, to some, all the more horrible because it had been written by a bishop. *Honest to God* rapidly reprinted seven times and sold hundreds of thousands of copies. It was a phenomenon.

And so began a trend towards the popular debunking of traditional doctrines, and Bishop Robinson followed up his smash-hit success with the even more iconoclastic paperback *But That I Can't Believe* which, he declared, was written with the express purpose of teaching the new theology to readers of tabloid newspapers. It all came along in the breathless rush of the 1960s and it was seen by many as the theologians' and the Church's contribution to the general climate of 'liberation' in which we were reckoned to be excitingly enveloped: though, as Chesterton had pointed out a generation earlier, it is hard to see how, to put it at its mildest, the discouragement of historical belief could be described as a sign of new freedom for anyone. As T S Eliot said, 'A people without history is not redeemed from time'.

All the miracle stories of the New Testament and so, by implication, the doctrines of the Creeds, were 'reinterpreted' in mythological or psychological terms. So the Virgin Birth was said to be a typical example of the sort of legend which, among the unenlightened and the primitive, came to surround influential personages, to which company Jesus Christ was generously allowed to belong. The bodily Resurrection was dismissed as one of the things that Bishop Robinson, and so by extension all thoughtful people — with the possible exceptions of such as St Paul, St Augustine and St Thomas Aquinas — could no longer bring themselves to believe. And so the Resurrection was psychologised to mean, 'The new life which the apostles experienced after Christ's death' — while the origin and cause of this sensation of new life was left unanalysed in the primitive darkness. And so with the Ascension, the Second Coming and all the other articles of faith — all dispatched with a smart wink and a shifty nudge along with the stories about walks on the water and the multiplication of loaves and fishes.

Relativising morality: love as 'feel good'

Inevitably, the doctrinal Deformation extended to the realm of morality. Chapter Six of *Honest to God* was about Situation Ethics, a fashionable ecclesiastical brand of act-utilitarianism in which good and right are not assessed by rule-keeping (or Ten Commandments-keeping) but by whether a particular action is 'the loving thing to do in the circumstances'. This begged the question of how the moral agent might come to know what the loving thing is without tried and tested rules and guidelines. It quickly came to mean that what feels right is right — a doctrine scarcely different from that of another famous Chapter Six: that in A J Ayer's tract on logical positivism *Language, Truth and Logic* (1936). In 1963, Honest John Robinson was singing the same song as The Beatles': *All You Need Is Love.* But 'love' defined without reference to established codes and traditional practice becomes a dislocated thing and the only criterion for its appearance is feeling. 'This is right' was translated without remainder into 'This feels right' — as good a definition of gaseous sentimentality as might be found.

A historical religion without any traditional restraints

Within a very few years, beliefs and morals had become detached and what passed for contemporary understanding of the Christian faith was, and is, an airy, insubstantial thing, a collection of indulgent sentiments in the presence of some old stories and some 'nice' feelings about one's fellow man — if not always about the man of flesh and blood who lives next door.

Sentimentality as a genre derives partly from Romanticism; and it is the romantic prejudice which enthrones the individual. So Situation Ethics were not about what *any* reasonable person ought to do in particular circumstances, but triumphantly about what *I* — pale copy of the Romantic hero though I be — am commanded to do by the way I feel. In the 1970s and 1980s, secular politics rediscovered the concept of the Individual as the locus of economic, social and moral authority; and in the 1990s the Individual as consumer is sovereign. But this Individual, deprived of rules, doctrines and an authoritative tradition, is a law unto himself only; and this self, unfixed, unshaped and unconstrained — to which must be added, in the absence of a tradition of thought and practice, uneducated — by the general laws and procedures is the exquisite captive of his own desires and whims: a bundle of shifting sentimental attachments.

Churchy sentimentality tries to be exciting

One might have expected the Evangelical wing of the Church to resist this sentimentalising tendency. True, Evangelicalism itself has historically set much store by emotional commitment of the sort found in Wesley's revival in which a million and more English hearts were 'strangely warmed'. But the temptation to emotional excess was always tempered by the strong sense of doctrine, by the belief that ardent religious affections should be in the service of truth spelt out by propositional revelation and the authority of Scripture. The old-style Evangelicals were noted for their biblical understanding and for their doctrine of revealed authority on which that understanding was based. The best antidote to the gush and froth of sentimentality is substantive content, something real and authoritative, the word made flesh: and this is precisely what saved Evangelicals from spurious religiosity — their high doctrine of Scripture, the conviction that there is something more solid and binding than the deceitful affections.

Unfortunately, the new-style Evangelicals in the happy-clappy Charismatic Movement are unhampered by such traditional constraints. Visit any Charismatic act of worship and you will come away thinking that, to Bishop Robinson's *All You Need Is Love* has been added *Anything Goes*.

Visit our local Anglican Charismatic Church here in York any Sunday evening and you will be accosted by many startling impressions, the chief of which is a sort of predetermined formlessness. Only the Medieval stone walls and the eighteenth-century religious portraits reassure the visitor that he has in fact entered a church. The milieu is like that of the pop-concert as early-arriving members of the 'audience' stroll among the pews, calling out, 'Hi!' to friends and acquaintances and pausing now and then to hug one another flamboyantly. All the body-language is over-inflected in a style which would seem insincere even on the theatrical stage. This supercharged emotionality can hardly be genuine. One would be ill from it, if it were — as from an excess of chocolates or a surfeit of lampreys. But it is not genuine. It is sentimental.

No organ music for introit. No robed clergy or choir. Nothing at all to let the alien know the service has begun. The designer-scruffy impresario who turns out to be lead-singer in the rock band bawls into the microphone in his transatlantic accent, 'I wanna teach you a new song ...' The overhead projectors reveal the doggerel of this first song and the noise starts. The impression is of audience-participation at the Christmas pantomime at York Theatre Royal. It is a long way from, 'O Lord open thou our lips'.

The words of this song, and all the songs, are so vacuous as to be almost meaningless. The congregation sways from side to side and does its best to look like the audience at a rock concert. Many take little notice of the proceedings at all, but continue to wander about the place, gesticulating to acquaintances, stopping off here and there for the stylised hug. The mind — an unusual spectator at this feast — casts around for some vestige of form in the formlessness and finds itself at last falling into the recognisable rhythms only of its own recollections; and these turn out to be a definition of what is going on:

> Shape without form, shade without colour,
> Paralysed force, gesture without motion ...

Another impresario in a pullover featuring a commercial design stands up to give the notices and to publish the banns of marriage. It is all done hurriedly, as if the speaker is ashamed of this little piece of unavoidable conventionality. This is the only vestige of structure in the whole show. He prays that those to be married, '...may know the whole joy and fullness of marriage *from the very start*'. The alien, the sceptic, asks himself, 'How could they — except by a sentimental reduction of the whole concept of matrimony and the purposes for which it was ordained?'

A round, bearded man in a jumper which prompts recollections of circumnavigation preaches the sermon. But this was not a sermon as we recall sermons: it was a series of in-jokes to massage the egos of his audience, his coterie: 'Paul was against circumcision. The Judaisers said you had to be circumcised to be saved. That rules out half the human race. Think about it. Not for too long though — it could be sinful!' The whole performance is characterised by this sort of desiccated sexual innuendo. They snigger and nudge one another in the pews.

Sentimentality in worship as insincere friendliness: pullovers, hugging and pax

The big, bearded man in the Magellan pullover — suddenly we realise he is the Vicar — interrupts himself: 'Let's have a break. You know, I see all sorts of things from up here. Burgeoning romances. Hands moving towards each other across the pew — not mentioning any names ...' His theme is, self-defeatingly, 'The Gospel plus anything else is not the Gospel'. No? Not even the Gospel plus smutty jokes and spoilt music? He requires 40 minutes to get over his point about spurious additions. The sermon is followed by more of the spoilt music and banal choruses repeated so many times that the visitor, the alien, begins to feel dizzy. It is all content-free, insubstantial, and its evident purpose is to foster a rootless, nebulous togetherness. But why repeat something 20 times which was not worth singing once? A few begin to twitch and jabber, and others jig about a bit; but most only look mildly bored. Even sentimentalists seem to guess when they are being overfed with sentimental cues. One is reminded of the fifth circle of hell inhabited by those with hollow eyes and all passion spent.

They would say that they are communicating the Gospel in a style uncluttered by the trappings of tradition, in a form that is 'accessible' to 'young people'. But when these middle-aged ecclesiastical rockers say such things they deceive themselves. Nothing is being communicated except a sentimental-paranoiac proclamation of the superior, privileged status of the Charismatic in-group. Bonding ceremonies for the like-minded.

Charismatic worship is the very definition of sentimentality as free-floating, uncritical emotionality: one clean blast of godly irreverence blows it all away. It is not, however, quite true to say that the Emperor has no clothes. He has: that voluminous woolly pullover, some cast-offs from the age of flower-power, the trappings of the stand-up comedian long past his best and enough smiling unctuousness to fill the closet of Uriah Heep.

Lord Runcie, the former Archbishop of Canterbury, has recently criticised these happy-clappy services for their lack of rootedness and substantial content. Without traditional form and substance, he says, religious response is bound to be merely sentimental — what we would like to feel if at all times we could choose our feelings. Why strive for it? Some claim Prozac provides this satisfaction without the need to turn out on a wet night. The impression is of a blasphemous sham. The Church is commanded by Christ to teach, and teaching requires the putting-in of substantial verities. Why does 'indoctrination' carry only the negative sense in the 1990s? Of course, as Pilate knew, truths are contestable; but contest and debate must be by means of public language, and must involve issues of form and content. But in the sentimentality of Charismatic worship, substance is void and language is not the means of debate or instruction but the method and code of emotional manipulation — the manufacture of feeling which is sentimentality's trademark. As for truth's 'accessibility', C H Sisson has remarked, 'There is no such thing as noble truth communicated in ignoble words'.

The new liturgies are sentimental and euphemistic

What need has the English Church to go slumming into the mid-Atlantic inflections of the chat-show presenters and the spurious argot of pop lingo when it possesses a 400-year tradition, a near monopoly of religious vocabulary, in the words of *The King James Bible* and *The Book of Common Prayer*? Lord Runcie, who now sees so clearly how far we have fallen, did nothing to prevent the tumble in the first place. In fact, it was his foot which kicked away the ladder when he put his whole archiepiscopal weight behind the *Alternative Service Book* (1980). By so doing, he made it certain that the whole Church — not just the Evangelical and Liberal factions — would become stranded in the shallows of sentimentality.

The *ASB* is a kind of long-running definition of sentimentality. Its euphemistic phrases sponge and dab away all the rootedness of the earthy *BCP*. The authors and supporters of the *ASB* have made a career out of disparaging the old Prayer Book for its alleged 'irrelevance', but what they have put in its place is so attenuated and effete as to be of no earthly use to anyone. Leave aside for a moment Sunday Services which are attended only by a few, and turn to the occasional offices which, in an established Church, still offer rites of passage to all and sundry.

At once we notice that sentimentality is not only an effete quality, but a *style*: it is patronising and babyish, Noddy language, and above all cosy. For example, what used to be called 'The Solemnisation of Matrimony' is now only 'The Marriage Service'. Don't they believe that our marriages are solemn any longer, or what? 'The Marriage Service' is like that other misbegotten production of the liturgical revolution, 'Family Services'. It is the togetherness language of the advertising industry — as if the parson were all the time saying, 'Don't miss this special offer for all the family!' The new rite is a sentimental parody of the original as it omits all the earthy expressions such as 'sin', 'fornication', 'men's carnal lusts and appetites'. Those words used to warn us that sex is dangerous and that human desires can be fickle. But now Happy Families has replaced 'this holy estate' and all is sentimentally suffused in the costless, happy glow of the Pelagian bourgeoisie praying to its kindly God. Wine into water.

When from 'The Marriage Service' all those stern but reassuring words about matrimony as 'a remedy against sin and to avoid fornication' are omitted, we can only assume that the Church no longer condemns sin (though not, of course, the sinner) and that what has been for centuries regarded as essential Christian doctrine is now, in this bland, inoffensive and sugary rite, repealed, revoked or otherwise cast aside. It is the Church's doctrine of human nature which has been emasculated and sentimentalised here, because it is no longer seen as good form to suggest that this nice modern couple of consumers at the chancel steps might be capable of sin. Actually, in the sentimental 1990s, adultery and fornication are rife and one marriage in three ends in divorce. A good opportunity then for the parson to address the couple in the words of the stern injunction from the *BCP*:

> I require and charge you both, as ye will answer at the dreadful day of judgement when the secrets of all hearts shall be disclosed ...

The censorship of judgement

But the *ASB* prescribes no such thing. That the official liturgy of the Church of England omits all reference to the day of judgement should really come as no surprise: liturgists who can abolish 'sin' and replace 'the fear of God' with 'serious thought' will have no trouble doing away with Christ's prophecies about the end of the world and the certainty of God's judgement upon sinners. And so, 'I require and charge you both' becomes the inoffensive and apologetic aside, 'I am required to ask'. Note the weakness of that passive voice as it betrays a loss of nerve. 'I require' is a challenge. 'I am required' might be a notice from the Council Tax Office or the Inland Revenue. The demoralised character of the new marriage service refuses to accept that the bride and groom are fallen creatures always liable to sin. They look so chic and the wedding — or at least the reception — is going to be so expensive that it would be bad form to risk offending them with reminders about human frailty. Instead there is effusiveness and sentimental gush: 'In delight and tenderness' and 'All that I am I give to you' — saccharin words, fit only for the Hollywood crooner or *Four Weddings and a Funeral*.

Tepid sensuality. But when it comes to real flesh, the *ASB* takes fright — especially when the flesh happens to be deceased. The sentimental ambience that produced the new funeral rite does not like to dwell on too solid flesh, and liturgists who had so little time for corporeality when it was animated will have even less to do with it when it is demised. Consider that proud, confident statement which the minister used to pronounce as he led the coffin down the aisle: 'I know that my Redeemer liveth'. Those are defiant words of faith made more faithful by the music of Handel's *Messiah*. Here comes a parson leading a corpse and yet he speaks of redemption. The dramatic effect is breathtaking: in the midst of death, we are in life. Surely it is the business of liturgy to fasten upon such a powerfully reassuring image as this? So why does the *ASB* leave it out? The reason soon becomes clear: those words are followed by, 'though after my skin worms destroy this body'. Ugh! You can just see the new brand of sentimental cleric holding his nose. And a book that dare not mention 'fornication' and 'carnal lusts' will hardly bring itself to a remembrance of 'worms'. But the forfeiting of the line about worms means that the profound faith of the next and final line must be given up as well. So the *ASB* cannot say (as the *BCP* said), 'Yet in my flesh shall I see God'. This omission reveals a loss of nerve which in turn reveals something much more serious: the loss of faith. And a sentimental Church here fails in its proclamation of the resurrection of the dead because it is too squeamish to speak of death in the first place. But if they dare not tell us of earthly things, why should we believe them when they speak of heaven?

Omitting morality

If there is a phrase better recalled than, 'I know that my Redeemer liveth' it is 'Earth to earth, ashes to ashes, dust to dust'. The *ASB* has not the emotional strength to utter these words, and so the Gospel itself — the good news of the resurrection from the dead — is once again emasculated by a wan and evasive sentimentality. It says, 'In appropriate cases, these words may be omitted'. When? What would constitute an appropriate case? These words make equal sense at the crematorium and at the graveside. The words immediately following in the *BCP*, 'who shall change our vile body' are also left out, of course. Vile bodies have no place in these obsequious obsequies. What, corpses at funerals? Whatever next! But the *BCP* mentions 'our vile body' so that in the very next line it can contrast this with the undying hope, 'that it may be like unto his glorious body'. And because the *ASB* omits the vileness, it must also omit the glory. Once again sentimentality, which is also an attempt to avoid genuine emotional disturbance, entirely emasculates the great Christian belief that dying we live. Sentimentality in doctrine and worship, far from rendering the Christian faith 'relevant' and 'accessible' — and pandering to the effete sensibility of a generation given to fashionable evasiveness and euphemism — actually corrodes spiritual truth and renders it ineffectual. No sin, no death, no vile bodies — so why all this fuss about forgiveness and resurrection?

Birth as well as death is sentimentalised in the new services
The child is introduced to the world of churchly sentimentality at his baptism. In the *ASB* rite, there is no mention of the fact that 'all men are conceived and born in sin' (*BCP*) — my God, that wouldn't look nice on the gooey invitations! — or of those other telling phrases, 'the old Adam', 'crucify the old man' and 'the devil and all his works'. The devil is not even mentioned, let alone renounced. All reference to the Ten Commandments is left out. The revisers do not see that, by playing down the idea of sin, they make the doctrine of regeneration of no effect. And so Holy Baptism — but the word 'holy' is not used on the title-page — is in the *ASB* no longer beautiful, awe-inspiring — the place of holy water in the mystical washing away of sin — but only pretty, a sentimental prelude to the booze-up and the cake, an opportunity for photographs and now *video obbligato:* but photographs and a video that will evidence *what*?

Traditional Christianity is robust and unsentimental. It has no illusions about human depravity. The glory of it is that God loves us, bad as we are. The new sentimentality in religion glosses over our dark side, and therefore it is not only a doctrinal failure; it is psychologically inaccurate and so finally incoherent. We are not such stuff as we are portrayed in the modern liturgies and rites of passage. And this is not a judgement on mere style or emphasis: by misrepresenting human nature, the *ASB* actually perverts the Gospel.

Morning and Evening Prayer in the *ASB* have been sentimentalised so that there is no reference in the Confession to 'miserable offenders'. But we *are* miserable because of our offence — that is the Christian teaching. And in the Confession in the Holy Communion, we no longer 'acknowledge and bewail our manifold sins and wickedness', we have no longer sinned 'in thought, word and deed'; there is no mention of God's 'wrath and indignation' — and so all reference to his pardon is worthless. How cheap redemption is when there was never any possibility of hell! What are the revivalists — who also use the *ASB* — making such a fuss about?

We do not say of our sins, 'The remembrance of them is grievous unto us: the burden of them is intolerable'. All these things are far too 'downbeat' to mention. But is the age which has produced the concentration camps and Hiroshima really less sinful than the age of

Archbishop Cranmer? Shouldn't an age which prides itself on the fact that it has been taught by Sigmund Freud know that 'the remembrance of them is grievous unto us: the burden of them is intolerable' — because our sins and the guilt which corrupts us will not be wished away by sentimental musings, but will fester in the unconscious spiritual parts from which they will inconveniently burst forth in 'wrath and indignation' in the form of all kinds of neuroses and mental disturbance; and that the only cure for the soul is catharsis — precisely acknowledging and bewailing?

The Roman Catholic Church is part of the religious speakeasy

I write as a lifelong Anglican, but there is scarcely more reality to be discovered in what, until comparatively recently, was regarded as the Ark of True Religion: the Roman Catholic Church. Here also we see the same looking-glass world of self-parody taken to such extremes that it resembles the creation of the satirists. For example, there is a universal declaration for lay-involvement — 'Prayer is impossible without participation'; but this injunction to liturgical togetherness is instantly undermined by a simultaneous ban on traditional processions.

In the new politically-correct Church, even sentimentality faces tests of ideological orthodoxy: togetherness is desirable as a form of political solidarity at celebrations of the Mass for workers; but traditional forms of lay participation, such as the Corpus Christi processions are discouraged as 'primitive' and 'superstitious'. The workers are OK so long as they agree with the Commissar. Catholics of the world unite: you have nothing to lose but your traditions.

It is not only the devout RC peasantry who have been made victims of the new trend towards comfiness in religion: a prominent Church in Paris recently removed from before the Blessed Sacrament its *prie dieus* and instead installed thick pile carpets and armchairs. Customer care supplants penitence as the *mysterium tremendum et fascinans* is replaced by the easy moment of what is now called 'contemplative therapy'. But we only need therapy when we are sick. And, as Karl Kraus said, 'psychotherapy is the disease for which it pretends to be the cure'.

A sentimental miasma hangs over the Catholic Church as the old doctrine of the representative priest gives way to the new sanctimonious hooliganism of mass-participation. For example, prayers must be comprehensible in order to be valid; but the abolition of the Latin

Mass has made it unlikely that the millions of French tourists (to say nothing of the English) passing into Spain and Portugal every summer understand a word of the Holy Service.

Never mind, they can stay in Poitiers and enjoy the exquisite togetherness of last year's Festival Concelebration when huge quantities of bread and wine were consecrated indiscriminately and worshippers were invited to step forward and help themselves. Here, as everywhere, today's sentimental priest faces 'across the table' his familiar chums in the act of celebrating the Eucharistic Sacrifice. We are supposed to believe that the introversion created by this circular boundary somehow makes for inclusivity: it does not; it excludes by means of its chummy circumference.

The priest truly offers on behalf of the whole world of sinners when, with the people behind him, he faces the transcendence that lies beyond the east window. But for whom is the bread being broken in these emasculated rites? The Tridentine Church was not afraid of the scandal of particularity: '*Pro multis*', it said — the officiant not hesitating to announce that some, through unrepented sin, might exclude themselves. The new 'President of the Corporate Thanksgiving' has no brakes on his universalist cycle as he translates 'For many' as 'For all'.

We have already observed the attenuated form of the Solemnisation of Matrimony in the C of E. In the Roman Catholic Church it is worse. Nothing must be done to offend the delicately liberated sensitivities of Ron and Eth as they approach the chancel step. True, the prescribed Epistle for the Marriage Service insists that the first purpose of matrimony is procreation; but this reading is now declared 'optional' and Ron and Eth are free to create their own Mass and to substitute for the writing of the Holy Apostle any text or reading of their own choice which might enhance the gooeyness of the occasion.

I have always thought that the very title of the rite Extreme Unction declares something solemn and profound, barely approachable because, well, it *is* so extreme. But the modern Church has moderated the extremity as it now announces General Absolution for the Aged Sick. All they have to do, as it were, is throw away their crutches and their heart-lung machines and approach the gleaming stare of Fr Soroptimus who will then wave a genial hand of forgiveness over all. The ultimate has now become sentimentally penultimate. Penitence has been downgraded in the interests of a corporate euphemism.

Similarly, there was also recently announced a general amnesty for backsliders by which the lapsed and the half-hearted were welcomed back with the promise of the forgiveness of sins: 'All those present are invited to accept the Church's pardon for their past sins'. But when sins can be dismissed as easily as that, what price redemption? It was like an invitation to an excuse-me dance: cheap grace, as the Protestant Bonhoeffer said, now on offer.

Throughout the modern Catholic Church there is a genial, Pelagian, celebration of human niceness which chiefly means making everything easier for everybody. No one in authority seems to understand that this policy undervalues the pain of Christ's sacrifice: if forgiveness comes so easily, why was there traditionally all that emphasis on his suffering? The catastrophic irony of the new authorities' easy-going ambition has never been better expressed than by Archbishop Lefebvre:

> The Church prescribes free love for the laity and marriage for the clergy. If you perceive in this apparent illogicality an implacable logic having as its objective the ruin of Christian society, you are seeing things as they are and your assessment is correct.

Sentimentality denies the Incarnation

Sentimentality is that rosy, wishful-thinking which is not quite real. It is a humourless parody of reality. Reality with the bones taken out — the flesh and blood having been removed already. Sentimentality is, to use a Victorian word, a vapour. It offers us the world as Dingly Dell, in which everyone is neither more nor less than 'nice'. It believes in our intrinsic goodness — but no, to say 'believes' is to go too far. For belief implies hard thought and reasoning, the weighing of arguments. And sentimentality does not like to tax itself with overmuch thought, and it avoids argument as one of the class of things which are strenuous and therefore 'not nice'.

The trouble is, of course, that reality — the world, the flesh and the devil — cannot so easily be chased away by even the most diligent wishful-thinking or by the consumer-Pelagianism of our time. Reality intrudes. It is like an awkwardly-positioned stone on the most smoothed-out of paths, or like the statue of the Commendatore unexpectedly turning up and making 'judgmental' noises at Don Giovanni's barbecue. Reality, like cheerfulness, will insist on breaking in.

Consider the modern churchman as sentimental moralist and amateur politician. His first act in the identification of evil is to thrust the awful business as far away from himself and his little like-minded group as possible. So he will, after all, allow wickedness and evil; but these things are not 'my fault' and certainly not 'my own most grievous fault': evil is *their* fault; it is supremely the fault of 'the system'. Well, we were warned by T S Eliot in 1934 that the defining characteristic of the *bien pensant* sentimentalist is always to be 'dreaming of systems so perfect that no one will need to be good'.

And so from his baptism (unhampered by satanic attendance), from his photogenic nuptials (unthreatened by inconvenient lust) and before his death (summarily described as without body, parts or passions) the contemporary Christian spokesperson escapes into the political life. This act shadows the divine condescension as the 1990s technological Marcionite — the archetypal synodsman — deigns to involve himself in the dirty affairs of the *res publica*. And it *is* a dirty business. Politicians — at least when they are out of earshot of their advertising agents — have to deal with the real world, the world with all the bones left in; the world of offences and injustices, inequalities and sectional interests. This world is easy to understand for the modern churchman, no longer washed in the blood of the Lamb, but at least accustomed to the lick and promise offered by the flannel and cheap grace of contemporary liturgies. He is such an authority, this modern churchperson, so recently descended from the realm of pious euphemism and sentimentality that he is instantly able to assimilate all the pernickety and intractable problems of practical politics to the universal balm of his innocent generalities.

From divine love to campaigns against the arms trade

He knows that all peoples, races and languages should love one another, and so he immediately translates, without hindrance of particularity, this godly doctrine into the sentimental declaration that, for example, Britain should not export arms. But it is his uncritical, sentimental adoption of 'peace' motives that makes him refuse armaments to small nations which are being oppressed by larger ones; to people in the right against those in the wrong. And so a sentimental attitude based on a facile and uncritical — *hypo*critical — theory of peace and justice for all is likely to lead only to war and oppression and to the greater suffering of the innocent.

And on the domestic scene the sentimental Christian spies poverty and hardship. The instincts of his forefathers would have been to give of their own personal wealth to charity for the specific alleviation of poverty. But, at least since the times of Charles Dickens, we have been taught to regard that most excellent virtue, that most warm-hearted thing, as 'cold charity'. For which, once again for the sentimentalist, the remedy must be a reformation of 'the system'.

In this case 'the system' means economic policy. And if economics falls short of being an exact science, it is at least a knack — something which requires training and expertise. But the sentimental Christian spokesperson is content to take refuge again in generalisations and theorising. He looks at the poor and he looks at the relatively well off and straight away draws a caricature: the rich should pay the poor, and this is best done through a policy of high taxation. But, as ever, the sentimentalist ignores the awkward particulars and heads straight for the magnificent generalisation. His enthusiasm for higher taxes for the rich and for, as Bishop Sheppard has called them, 'the comfortable', has blinded him to the fact that, in the real world, 'rich' and 'poor' are not merely emotive slogans but approximate and relative terms which merge into each other: specifically, that to ensure a sufficient revenue from taxation alone to help the poor might paradoxically and counter-productively involve taxing the poor themselves. And this is a conclusion which politicians increasingly draw about welfarism in general.

Rosiness versus reality

These self-defeating notions are just what we have come to expect of sentimentality whose essence and definition is the rosy misperception, and sometimes the deliberate evasion, of reality. The remedy for sentimentality is in Christianity itself which is a most unsentimental, fleshly and rooted faith. The Christian faith does not shrink from looking at the world as it is, and not as we might like it to be. What would be the use of religion as a soroptimistic gloss? It does not seek to evade, excuse or euphemise human frailty, but actually provides a cure for it — through suffering. Christianity is not attenuated idealism and pious waffle. God in Christ took on the world on its own terms, condemned it and then redeemed it: not by a process of sentimental excuses but by himself coming right down to earth and earthy involvement with humankind. Sentimentality is the flesh translated into pious verbiage. The antidote to sentimentality is the Word made flesh.

7

Faking emotion

sentimentality in modern literature

Ian Robinson

Working off feelings on yourself, feelings you haven't really got

Sentimentality was one of the preoccupations of the great English generation of the 1920s, so it should not be surprising that the essential work on the concept is to be found in D H Lawrence and T S Eliot and then in their pupil F R Leavis. Lawrence's definition should be standard:

> It is when he comes to sex that Mr Galsworthy collapses finally. He becomes nastily sentimental. He wants to make sex important, and he only makes it repulsive. Sentimentalism is the working off on yourself of feelings you haven't really got. We all *want* to have certain feelings: feelings of love, of passionate sex, of kindliness, and so forth. Very few people really feel love, or sex passion, or kindliness, or anything else that goes at all deep. So the mass just fake these feelings inside themselves. Faked feelings! The world is all gummy with them. They are better than real feelings, because you can spit them out when you brush your teeth; and then to-morrow you can fake them afresh.[1]

But what could it mean to call an emotion fake? What would make you suspect an emotion is faked? Commonsense will reply that we just do know whether we are feeling something or not, and the question whether it's genuine feeling doesn't arise unless one is crazy or drunk. Even with drunken emotions people sometimes know that they *are* drunk and take that into account. The possibility of taking intoxication into account, however, immediately confirms the possibility of judging that there may be something not genuine about a feeling.

Pretending to feeling

The first sign that Lawrence is on to something is that even if we are confident enough to deny faked feelings in ourselves, one can hardly live in our world without noticing them in others and especially in public. It is hardly possible to open a newspaper without coming on a report of somebody's 'signalling' strong feeling. *Fury, outrage,* are (thank God) not often met with outside the columns of the newspapers, typeset by journalists reporting politicians who are not even suspected of harbouring these feelings. 'What is your reaction to this shooting, Minister?' 'It is one of horror.' As Collingwood remarks, a poet never *names* the emotions he is expressing. We know for certain that whatever the minister is feeling, if anything, he is not horrified. If there is anything in any of these reports, the public figures reported are pretending to have feelings for the sake of their public 'image', a word that itself suggests a fake. The only question here is whether the minister is even bothering to fake the feeling, for there is an odd sense in which these displays of public feeling are not even meant to take anyone in. Some Victorians writing letters of condolence would scatter water on to the paper to smudge the ink. These imitation tears were scarcely more of a claim to real feeling than the use of black-bordered writing paper.

The feelings exhibited at party conferences are sometimes so evidently manipulated that one suspects that the true emotion, if any, belongs to the manipulation. Emotions are choreographed, as when, at the 1996 Republican convention, a little girl with AIDS 'read from the tele-prompter, "My dreams are a little different from others. I dream of a cure for Aids."' 'Then came Mrs Reagan. As reported in the (English) *Daily Telegraph*: 'Party weeps over Reagan's long goodbye' subtitled 'Brave speeches bring show of compassion from delegates'.[2] This often hard-bitten journal seems to believe that the emotions do really exist, but couldn't avoid the word 'show' and mentions the tele-prompter. The even more hard-bitten *Financial Times* did better, the same day, with 'Laughs and tears right on cue in made-for-TV convention', and made the called-for remark about the response to the tribute to Mr Reagan, 'Grown men were shown weeping. Finally, the convention organizers had successfully struck their chosen chord: nostalgia.' Emotion indicated like notes in a musical score. But whether a chord actually expresses emotion will depend on the music. NB, it is not being said that there is nothing very sad about poor Mr Reagan's condition, that we cannot feel for him, or that he was not a great man; but that the playing of emotions as on a keyboard introduces falsity. For instance those in the audience who happened not to be weeping must have been tempted to try.

Faked public emotions include the well-scripted outbursts from mothers with daughters kidnapped or recently dead from drugs, who occasionally even give the impression of making the most of a one-and-only chance of fame. What would true emotion be like in the circumstances? Quite unpredictable, unscriptable. In politics and religion, sentimentality maintains its classic alliance with hypocrisy. It sometimes seems that the feeling of the contemporary Church of England could be summed up in the prayer 'O God, Bosnia!', from clerics who have vague feelings about Bosnia but no knowledge, even if they have been there. Here sentimentality does its usual work of inhibiting judgement. The same clerics will pray with easy feeling for the homeless and the outcasts before passing them by on the other side on their way home to dinner.

Faked public emotion is less common in England, however, than the other extreme: efforts are made to exclude emotion from 'efficient' politics. Politicians are warned that emotionality can lose votes, and those with bad tempers, like Mr Michael Heseltine, are afraid of losing them in public and sounding 'over the top'. So they will preface some irrational statement or other by saying that we must judge calmly and by reason, and not let our emotions run away with us. The opposition of reason (granting them as much) and emotion, and the assumption that the suppression of emotion will improve reason, raises a large and interesting historical question, which I will glance at below. Either way in contemporary politics, emotion or reason normally sound mechanical and therefore faked, for reason is no more a mechanism than feeling.

A feeling must be judged a fake if we really can't imagine anyone holding it. Local newspapers keep ready-made *In Memoriam* verses for the use of customers who want to express in public their feelings about the departed. These are usually deliberately badly written, with rhymes that don't quite rhyme or lines that don't quite scan, to suggest the artless simple feeling straight from the heart of the folk. Modern newspaper readers are not peasants and, again, I am sure nobody really credits these feelings. It doesn't follow that anyone using these ready-made verses has no feelings, or even that they cannot use these verses to express feeling to themselves. But any feelings there may be cannot be expressed in the common language to the rest of us; they are not *in* these verses. The verses are themselves insincere.

> Each night we say a little prayer
> And ask the Lord above,
> To put his arms around you Grandad
> And give you all our love.

There was, presumably, a space at the end of the third line. Mum or Dad would have scanned better, but girlfriend or partner would go equally well. It would no doubt be too literal minded to ask whether this family actually prays in this fashion every night. The question is what they think they are doing by paying the paper a few pounds to print the lines, and the only answer can be: expressing emotions which the words cannot carry.

We are faking it because we speak a fake language

But if the feelings we lay claim to are not our real feelings must we not be mad? Well, perhaps we are, or perhaps the world is. Madness need not be only in individual pathology: it may have something to do with the world and language. If we have no language for our feelings the feelings we do express may not be the ones we really feel. If the language goes mad all feelings are wrong.

There are, then, links between faked feelings, the state of the whole language and culture, and common judgement. Deliberately insincere feelings are less common, let's hope, than the insincerity we can't help because of the state of the language. Anything is insincere if inauthentic, if it cannot sincerely be embraced. Judgement does have to come into any questions about sincerity and sentimentality.

Emotion itself is a kind of judgement, if it is a reaction to something. 'Over-reacting' notices a judgement of what is itself a judgement. But can there be such things as right feeling, right judgement?

All sentimental feeling is ill-judged but not all inappropriate emotion is sentimental. As well as ill-judgement sentimentality needs the element of *forcing* an emotion upon oneself, or of persuading oneself of feeling it.

Their place in history made sentimentality of special interest to Lawrence and Eliot, coming as they did at the end of the Victorian age. Sentimentality has a distinguished history. It is not very old in English. The question of authorial sentimentality doesn't really arise in Chaucer or Shakespeare. Chaucer's Prioress is sentimental, but there is no sentimentality in the depiction of her. The Pardoner's tear-jerking sermon, that might later have been a cue for sentimentality, is shown clearly as hypocrisy. Falstaff's fits of religiosity perhaps go deeper but are also well judged.

We naturally associate sentimentality with the Victorian age, with all those sugary-sweet pictures, distortions of any ordinary judgement of the world, that sometimes now fetch such surprising sums at auction. This is right enough, but the more remarkable thing that we see all over the Victorian age is a *split*. George Eliot, possibly the sharpest as well as the most formidable intellect of her age, dissolves, embarrassingly often, into tearful gushing. Words like her favourite *burthen, yearning, sobbing*, are traps into which this very 'strong-minded woman' plunges. For instance in the Positivist anthem, 'O may I join the Choir Invisible', by way of the rather wooden movement of the blank verse (did she, like the late Professor Donald Davie, have to count the syllables on her fingers?) she hopes for conditional immortality for

> all our rarer, better, truer self
> That sobbed religiously in yearning song,
> That watched to ease the burthen of the world.

Sobbing religiously in yearning song exactly fits Lawrence's definition of working off upon oneself feelings one hasn't got. Not that this great woman had no feelings, but they somehow get distorted and made vague in the expression, and she can lay claim to them only by switching off her intelligence.

Dickens has his own brand of this split, which can be shown in a text-book way by putting the beginning of the second chapter of *Bleak House* alongside the third. Introducing Sir Leicester Dedlock, Dickens is incisive though not altogether unsympathetic, clear-headed, sardonic. Then, having switched off the sardonic intelligence, he forces Esther Summerson upon himself and gushes. Thackeray will veer almost paragraph by paragraph from cynicism to tearfulness. In these cases it is always the emotional bits, never the satirical, that are false or faked. (Dickens was so determined to force decent feeling upon himself and his readers that he even sometimes persuaded himself he had expressed a love for homes full of squalling children.)

The extraordinary split, whereby to release emotion so many intelligent people had to shut off their intelligence, is part of what T S Eliot meant by the 'dissociation of sensibility'. In the prose age established at the end of the seventeenth century, things like George Eliot's throbbings and yearnings were banished from prose, and enthusiasm was equated with madness. The succeeding 'age of reason' could find no place for religious emotion, and John Wesley had to rebuke his open-air congregations when they went into fits. They had no other release (apart from the art of Charles Wesley's hymns). The Victorian age, still very much a prose age, the first great age both of railways conveying goods and of newspapers that conveyed information in a rather similar way, could only allow emotion as a safety-valve release during which the intelligence was turned off.

Serious writing requires irony. Sentimentality is unironic

Lawrence and Leavis did their work so well that at first glance it may seem that sentimentality need no longer be an issue for poets, dramatists and novelists. Is there still sentimentality left in poems and stories and plays? Well, plenty, of the ordinary kind, and in the classical line from our Victorian elders. The mark, now as then, is the lapse into unreality.[3]

> MYXOMATOSIS
> Caught in the centre of a soundless field
> While hot, inexplicable hours go by
> *What trap is this? Where were its teeth concealed?*
> You seem to ask.
>   I make a sharp reply
> Then clean my stick. I'm glad I can't explain
> Just in what jaws you were to suppurate:
> You may have thought things would come right again
> If you could only sit quite still and wait.

Larkin's first line is all right: for the poor deaf rabbit the field will be soundless. The possible trap in 'inexplicable' (for what explanations can be made to a rabbit?) is at least allowed for with 'seemed'. But with the so well-crafted last two lines, coming down so deliberately from the expertly inserted polysyllables of 'inexplicable' and 'suppurate' to two lines made almost entirely of monosyllables evidently meant to express simply decent Wordsworthian emotion, the poet actually sinks into the sentimentality possible when he turns off his intelligence. The rabbit could not have thought any such thing. Its plight is quite bad enough without the poet attributing human endurance to the animal. The rabbit's sitting quite still and waiting is actually sadder because no such thought was possible to it. Larkin is of course very accomplished, which makes his sentimentality interesting. He has succeeded in pulling the wool over his own eyes.

The mechanics of sentiment in the modern writer: Iris Murdoch

I used to think that the leading modern example of the dissociation of sensibility is the novels of Iris Murdoch, for at first sight (the only sight they usually get from me) they fall apart into the old divisions as neatly as George Eliot, though without her human interest. Sometimes Iris Murdoch writes sharply and intelligently. Then without any break she begins to gush. *The Sea, The Sea* (Winner of the Booker Prize, 1978) is, the blurb tells us, 'the story of an obsession' whose hero, Charles Arrowby, is 'driven by an obsessive passion'. The novelist has to try to reproduce this passion in English prose. This is first-person narrative, and at one point Charles Arrowby remarks, 'How high-flown, almost pompous, I am becoming, now that I am a prose-writer!'[4] — so pointing to the novelist's first line of defence, that this is dramatic monologue not omniscient narrator and so we may take it as ironically as need be. Of the first love whom he improbably rediscovers forty-plus years later, Charles declares, 'Ours was a solemn holy happiness, and we shunned the coarser talk of our schoolfellows.'[5] There is nothing to prevent us from giggling if we so wish. But is the invitation really intended by the novelist? If so did it really require 502 pages?

> I can see her smiling at me now. She was beautiful but with a secret beauty. She was not one of the "pretty girls" of the school. Sometimes her face looked heavy, almost dour, and when she cried she looked like the pig baby in *Alice*. She was very pale, and people sometimes thought she looked ill, although she was so strong and so healthy. Her face was rather round and white and her eyes gazed out with such a fey puzzled look, like a young savage. She had dark blue eyes which seemed to be violet when you were not looking at them. Her pupils were often dilated so that her eyes became almost black. She had very fine straight hair in a long bob. Her lips were pale and always cold; and when, with my eyes closing, I touched them so childishly with mine, a cold force pierced me like a spear, such as a pilgrim might feel when he knelt and touched some holy life-renewing stone. Her body was passive to my embraces, but her spirit glowed to me with a cold fire. Her beautiful shoulders ... [etc, etc][6]

The novelist whose irony is (unlike Jane Austen's) in doubt, risks the retort: she really means this rubbish! And there are those who would disagree with the judgement 'rubbish'. I expect it is this sort of passage the critic had in mind when grouping *The Sea, The Sea* with six 'mystic novels'.[7] What seems to me beyond serious dispute is that, in the old, useful distinction, this is all just (over)stated, not shown. No work is being done on language, nothing is really *made*. The fey puzzled look is pure Mills & Boon. The medieval cliché of the cold spear (only just rescued by Chaucer, beyond rescue in fluent modern prose) refuses to mix with the equally worn-out pilgrim image. The passage keeps falling into verse (*Her face was rather round and white, a cold force pierced me like a spear, some holy life-renewing stone*), sure sign of an attempt at deep significance that gets no further than the purple patch.

I nevertheless think I was wrong to think of Iris Murdoch as a simple descendant of the nineteenth-century split. The throbbings and yearnings and burthens of George Eliot are most unsatisfactory next to the wonderfully penetrating sympathy of her real art (the stories of Bulstrode, say, or Lydgate, or Gwendolen Harleth), but they are at least desperately in earnest. She stakes her all on the emotions, distorted or faked though they sometimes are. Iris Murdoch writes as purply as George Eliot at her most gushing, but the later purple is oddly mechanical and the novelist unimplicated. The attempt is being made to put something across, but what, quite, remains obscure because of the mechanical nature of the attempt. Mechanism, however, and cliché, certainly belong with the sentimental in Lawrence's thinking. The quoted bit of Iris Murdoch is bad writing of a fairly ordinary pulpy kind (and there is more where that came from): the reason for calling it *sentimental* is that it is quite unreal, gets no grip on life.

The best thing in *The Sea, The Sea* is actually the chapter of drunken talk between the hero and his friend Perry. Into this are inserted some intelligent notes about Ireland, the theatre, unhappy marriage — all in general, not with the local habitation of fiction, but the verve of the talk is well-maintained. Iris Murdoch can be an intelligent commentator, and has the gift of the gab; only she has no talent for fiction. My word-processor keeps trying to call her Irish Murdoch.

Alice Walker: sentimentality in the school curriculum

A much cruder transatlantic example, in which the author is wholeheartedly present (although before the book starts she tries to blame it on the Holy Spirit), is Alice Walker in *The Color Purple*.[8] This novel is worth mentioning because it is used as a set text for 'A'-level English, and on feminist courses in the British ex-universities, presumably as an example of modern novelistic thought and providing a morality for our modern world.

The Color Purple would be better called *The Black and the White*, for there are no intermediate shades. Black women are white, and men (except two who wisely accept female government), and most white women, irretrievably black.

If a male WASP had written *The Color Purple* he would have been accused of the 'Uncle-Tomming' (as the semi-literate Celie is made to call it,[9]) of condescending to the blacks (so Alice Walker refers to these human beings) as loveably stupid and primitive — though to be sure I don't myself find it quite loveable when one lady demonstrates her independence by sticking a table fork into her husband's hand and another by felling the mayor. But then there is Shug (short for Sugar) Avery, the magic woman, the queen bee, the salt of this earth. She rescues Celie from violence and slavery, loves her, tells her some facts about her sexuality, and sets her up making pants. She also has a lesbian affair with Celie, consequent upon a long-running affair with Celie's husband, but in middle age leaves her for a young man. Celie 'comes to terms with' this.

This is a sentimental, not an ordinarily stupid, novel, because Alice Walker, the signs are, knows what she's doing. The contrast of the comic-coon-nigger phraseology of Celie with the school-educated prose of her sister Nettie, reporting from Africa, is well maintained. But neither is authentic.

The novel is compulsively theological. Celie's first letters are addressed to God, but in the course of the fable her theology matures, under the guidance of Shug Avery. Celie asks 'What God do for me?' 'He gave you life, good health, and a good woman that love you to death,' answers Shug.

> Yeah, I say, and he give me a lynched daddy, a crazy mama, a lowdown dog of a step pa and a sister I probably won't ever see again. Anyhow, I say, the God I been praying and writing to is a man. And act just like all the other mens I know. Trifling, forgitful and lowdown.[10]

About the men in the novel Celie speaks no less than truth, from which we are to conclude that all men, and the anthropomorphic God with them, are trifling etc. (As a condemnation of the male sex as shown in

The Color Purple this is actually very mild. The story begins with the rape of Celie by the man she thinks is her father, though she is too innocent to know what is happening.) Shug rises to this challenge:

> Shug a beautiful something, let me tell you. She frown a little, look out across the yard, lean back in her chair, look like a big rose.
>
> She say, My first step from the old white man was trees. Then air. Then birds. Then other people. But one day when I was sitting quiet and feeling like a motherless child, which I was, it come to me: that feeling of being part of everything, not separate at all. I knew that if I cut a tree, my arm would bleed. And I laughed and I cried and I run all round the house. I knew just what it was. In fact, when it happen, you can't miss it. It sort of like you know what, she say, grinning and rubbing high up on my thigh.[11]

This is Wordsworthian, but a long way sub-Wordsworth. He too is not unsexual in his feelings about Nature; he actually does suffer as the result of the 'merciless ravage' he inflicts on the 'virgin scene' of the 'one dear nook' in that wonderful poem 'Nutting'; but he does not coarsen and generalise the feeling into the untruth that if one cuts a tree one's arm bleeds. 'Don't cant about savages', Johnson advised Boswell. Alice Walker is canting about savages. 'Blacks' are of course no more likely to be savages than whites: I refer to the characters in the novel, and the author's attitude to them.

Now: is the sentimentality of this novel found in its too facile emotion? or is it in the false judgements of human life that so satisfy the 'A'-level students and their examiners (below)? The interesting thing is that the unreal feelings and the unreal judgements fall together.

Indecent sentimentality: bad feelings can be phoney too

We ordinarily take sentimentality to be the working off on oneself of *decent* feelings one invents for the occasion, or the distortion of feeling into decency, but there is no need for the feelings to be decent. The eighteenth-century pornographical 'classic' *Fanny Hill* is a *very* sentimental novel, a faked Eden. If Galsworthy, as Lawrence says, tries to make sex important and only makes it repulsive, it could be said that Cleland tries to make orgies and promiscuity beautiful but only makes them sugary: he is able to do so by ignoring any part of sexual experience that might upset the rosy picture. The freedom from shame (which Lawrence himself offered in Lady Chatterley's simplified paradise), freedom from family connections, from children, from the pox, makes a world so unlike any real world as to involve the author's feelings in its unreality. Much the same goes for the other pornographical pseudo-classics I have sampled, including the Victorian periodical *The Pearl*, as sentimental as George Eliot's nobler yearnings.

Our Conservative-appointed Poet Laureate's most ambitious work, *Crow*, is sentimental in a comparable (though not this time obscene) reverse way. It lays claim to feelings and judgements that are just too low to be true. For Crow, aspraddle on the garbage, survival is the final virtue, and in the usual way the poet's intelligence, which would ask what makes Crow's life worth living, is switched off and Crow's continuing existence sentimentally, if disgustingly, celebrated.[12] Similarly, in Howard Brenton's play *The Romans in Britain*, the dwelling on nastiness is a kind of modern equivalent of the gothic horrors popular in Jane Austen's day, when girls like Catherine Morland in *Northanger Abbey* consoled themselves for the ordinariness of the modern world by imagining, with the help of Mrs Radcliffe, sanguinary horrors. The matter becomes serious for Catherine when her judgement lapses far enough for her to confuse the gothic with the real. In Brenton the confusion is the author's.

The commoner backlash against faked decent feelings is into a cynicism that can also be called sentimentality, because it is equally inauthentic.

The book jacket of Martin Amis's *London Fields* (1989) quotes recommendations of an earlier triumph, *The Rachel Papers*. 'Scurrilous, shameless ... ingenious obscenity, astute literariness, loathing, lust, anxiety ... fairly nasty'. It tells us much about judgement in the modern world if a publisher with a very distinguished record thinks 'fairly nasty ... ingenious obscenity' are phrases that will lead to sales. These comments, especially 'astute literariness', do apply to *London Fields*, as well as to the later and even more hyped novel *The Information* (1995). They amount to a reason for not bothering to finish either book. Why don't we all do something more pleasant? Life is really not like this!

London Fields is carefully and cleverly written in a manner that owes something to Henry James. Words are not only chosen with care: the care makes itself apparent to the reader, as one sometimes has to object to James, as an invitation to admire the cleverness. The difference from James is that there is no judgement in Amis's cleverness, and very little knowledge of life.

The compulsive nagging at D H Lawrence is symptomatic. (Cf the unfunny Howard Jacobson in *Coming from Behind*.) The modern cynic can no more leave Lawrence alone than the sentimental nineteenth-century unbeliever could leave God. Amis prints a parody of a famous passage of *The Rainbow*:

> He harkened to the chirrup of fruit-machine and the tolling of pinball table, humped the dodgy goods and defrayed life's pleasures with sweat of brow and groin and armpit, knew also the firm clasp of Analiese's ankles around his neck, the coarse reassurance of Trish Shirt's hair in his fist. And ever dazed from staring at the sun, the source of all generation. Heaven and earth was teeming around him. And how should this cease?[13]

Real mock-heroic works by allowing a glimpse of the authentic heroic amidst the deflation. This is only deflation, and becomes rapidly boring. Nothing teems in the world of this novel.

Sentimentality is cleverness without judgement

This may seem challengeable in view of the contempt with which most of the characters are presented. Keith, for instance, the womanising drunken hero of *London Fields*, whose life centres on darts, actually sees the world, the author tells us, in tabloid cliché,[14] and Mr Amis gives us some impeccably constructed examples.[15] These parodies are flawless but also lifeless. The effect cannot be to suggest such a vision of the darts as the dart-players hardly understand. When Mr Amis's novel sales collapse he will be able to make a living reporting football and darts, and there will be no way of knowing whether he is doing it tongue-in-cheek or not; there is *no difference* between his parody and the real thing.

The characters are such that in themselves nothing can be done with them, of which the author is fully aware. The same can be said for most of Ben Jonson's characters. The difference is that Jonson has a judgement and a fancy of invention that confers life and interest on his nonentities. In *London Fields* they remain inert, nagged at by the Jamesian precision of the phrasing which yet does nothing to bring them back to life.

'Unrelieved and cultureless banality' was one of Leavis's phrases for the world depicted by C P Snow. Nobody in *London Fields* has any belief, emotion, love, culture; nor are these supplied by the novelist. The characters are all at bottom bored with life, and, unlike Jonson, so is their author; but neither they nor Mr Amis will ever admit it. (Has Mr Amis read Roy Kerridge? The difference between *London Fields* and *Beside the Seaside* is that Kerridge does situate his culturelessly banal characters in a context of very funny judgement.)

The time and place is London after ten years of the Thatcher era, but London seen from a point of view that is so contemporary as to be out of time. It is of a particular time and place without being historical at all. It makes one begin to see Spengler's point, or even the current chatter about the end of history. Lawrence would have called it post-mortem, which I believe is strictly accurate provided one notices that the death is of the London Literary World, not of English. This is what a novel will be like after the life has finally departed from the life-form.

As to *The Information*, the novel which got Mr Amis into the literary gossip-columns for the size of the advance he received for it, reported as half a million pounds, I got to page 285, going slower and slower, and then stopped. This is not entirely Amis's fault, but mainly. It so happened that I was re-reading *Mansfield Park* at the same time. The contrast was painful. Jane Austen is an infinitely more entertaining comic novelist; she is also much wittier, because her wit is about actual human life. Compared with the circumscribed Regency spinster, Martin Amis knows nothing of life.

To say so is the same as to make the objection that his unemotionality is a fake. As Collingwood observes, there is *no* expression without feeling. This is an artificially cultivated deadpan which one really cannot attribute to a sentient being, and which therefore qualifies as a kind of reverse sentimentality.

Neither Iris Murdoch nor Martin Amis passes the first alive-or-dead test; the attention given to them by the academic establishment is itself a kind of sentimentality. We must have a literature, if only for the sake of keeping 'A'-level going, and so the academy works off upon itself the feeling that these novels are living works of literature. They aren't, and the pretence cannot be maintained for long.[16]

Cast adrift from common judgement by sentimentality

Thomas Cranmer, disgraced Archbishop of Canterbury, threatened with being burnt and knowing what that was like, for he had seen his dearest friends and allies suffer, made a series of increasingly abject recantations. At the very last, when he knew he would burn in any case, he recanted the recantations and died heroically. Which, if any, of the feelings he expressed were sincere, and how do we know? I think the question can be restated as: how can one make sense of what can be known of a whole life in its moment in history? Sincere feeling is authentic, it has to be believable, in its world. In this case, Cranmer being a master of expression, I am not in doubt that the true feeling was expressed in the university church at Oxford and at the stake.

True feeling, sincerity and authenticity, fall together — into art. Poetry is the touchstone. Leavis, in the essay referred to, distinguishes the feeling in poems by Emily Brontë and Thomas Hardy. Hardy's *Vestigia Veteris Fiammae* poems are full of feeling, simultaneously the convincing judgement of a life.

It should still be asked how we know. Judgement must judge the judge: what I think genuine will show you what I am. Critics always have to stick their necks out in judgements. I think much of the feeling in those Hardy poems is real and true. Much Wordsworth is genuine.

Thy friends are exultations, agonies,
And love, and man's unconquerable mind.

In the Sonnet to Toussaint it is important that Wordsworth associates the mind with extreme emotion. His real feeling is part of a reassociation of sensibility, a making life whole and able to be judged.

Convincingness

The challenge may be repeated: how do you know this is better than sentimentality? How do you know Wordsworth's feeling is genuine? Judgement is always challengeable, this side the last trumpet. But that doesn't mean it cannot be convincing. Poetry can be convincing — or unconvincing — if the whole man, the whole woman is brought in. I cannot prove that *King Lear* is a better play, truer, with more feeling, than Edward Bond's *Lear*, but I am in no doubt of the judgement and if need be will refer to it as a fact. It is another fact that the feeling in Iris Murdoch is fake, and so is the absence of feeling in Martin Amis. The trouble with writers like Martin Amis and Iris Murdoch is that in their different ways they have cast themselves adrift from the common judgement that says so.

Literature and criticism are internally related. Literature gets and is established by the criticism it deserves. Alice Walker gets set at 'A'-level to inspire criticism like the following, snippets from actual 'A'-level scripts leaked to me by a friend:

Love is the important thing in any way you can find to suit yourself and your partner/it doesn't matter what form it arrives in/whether of man or woman, your husband or lover/be it love for a person, love for an animal, or love for an object.

A religion that does not judge/God no longer the white man but a thing that is everywhere/a something, a beholder of beauty instead of the white ideas of an old white man with a white beard and white hair/ not a he but an it, pleased with creation.

This is at least as sentimental as a picture of an old man with a white beard. Celie was

far too sympathetic to others and careless of herself, too considerate, but she learns, through Shug Avery, to become more aggressive and self-seeking.

Everything comes together for her/she becomes strong/assertive/ aggressive/proud/a confident assertive woman who knows what and whom she wants/can finally live the life she wants/enjoy the lifestyle she wants/gets control of her own life/grows from being unhappy and unloved to someone who has gained what she wants/ finally happy to be herself, and not someone's wife/her husband's love for Shug highlights his weakness and this is important to Celie because it shows what a woman can do to a man and how she can treat him if she tries/learns much in her expressions of love and anger/the love she felt let her mouth off to him, and eventually stick a fork in his hand/this is the first real anger she feels.

I still have to say to the last comment: not real, *voulu*, wish-fulfilment, though not a wish I share; too far still from common judgement. The low-grade morality responds to the sentimentalized feeling; judgement and emotion both fall together into the 'aqueous, badly scented residue' Thomas Carlyle predicted would be left after the decomposition of religion. Criticism has to aim at sincerity, truth of feeling, and a common judgement fit to acknowledge Shakespeare; something better than the common judgement of those 'A'-level scripts.

Iris Murdoch has no grasp of the world, and neither has Martin Amis, and neither have these criticisms of Alice Walker, because none of them can get into their language the things George Eliot strove so hard for, seriousness about life, seriousness about the relations of the sexes and of individuals with the community, and the real feeling that cannot be separated. Lawrence and Leavis still have much to teach us.

8

The pity of self-pity

the sentimentalisation of music

Balint Vazsonyi

Composers used to have fun

'May this bring joy to the friends of humour, and annoyance to others', so the dedication reads of Ernö Dohnányi's *Variations on a Nursery Rhyme*. At its Berlin premiere in 1914, listeners were not amused. It took the London public to set the work on the path of success which continues world-wide in our days.

Yet the reasons for the composition's initial failure had more to do with the spirit of the times than the venue. In the eighteenth century, humour in music was everywhere. Most notable examples may be found in the symphonies of Joseph Haydn (and not only in the famous 'Surprise'), in Mozart's Shakespearean comedies, or in Beethoven's 'Fury over the lost penny'. Apparently, Mozart had fun, even, *with* music in his impudent financial venture under the title, 'To compose without the least knowledge of Music so much [sic] German Walzer or Schleifer as one pleases, by throwing a certain Number with two Dice'. In it, the divine spirit which had given us Don Giovanni and the Jupiter Symphony is applied to numbered one-bar segments that may be combined any-which-way to produce a unique 16-bar dance.

The sense of humour we encounter in that greatest blossoming of music-as-a-high-art was pure — that is, free of irony, sarcasm, mockery. And when it came to tragedy, that, too, was pure and grand — devoid of pettiness, misery and, above all, self-pity. Even Schubert, sad, unappreciated Franz Schubert stopped short of self-pity. *Winterreise* begins in a state of desperation and proceeds downhill from there. Yet, even as tragedy becomes personal, it does not cease to be Art.

The Italian tradition

Perhaps it was so because, in the eighteenth century, music still looked upon sunny Italy as its native land. No matter how much the German genius for infusing music with complex intellect had come to dominate the scene, no matter how extensive the encroachment of instrumental music over opera, Mozart was still steeped in the Italian tradition. Schubert, too, showed unmistakable signs of it.

Beethoven, for much of his life, continued to use the standard Italian designations for tempo or character. Then, in his last creative period, he needed something more personal. So, those sonatas and string quartets which, to this day, convey the most profound thoughts and sentiments ever expressed in music, often come with instructions in German, such as *'Gesangvoll, mit innigster Empfindung'* (Like singing, and with heart-felt sentiment). Yet as if to acknowledge his continuing debt to Italy, we suddenly find not only a new emphasis on singing, but the actual words *'Arioso'* and *'Arietta'* at heads of movements in piano sonatas.

I make so much of Italy, because I had made so much of humour. By the time Beethoven and Schubert depart, alone Rossini writes humour — infectious and irresistible — in music. Germany now embarks on creating the German opera and Weber's *Freischütz* fills the hearts and minds with hope, confidence, ambition. Richard Wagner is but one step away.

The importance of being 'genius'

Slowly, Italy (along with humour) was banished from 'serious' music. The palette of nineteenth-century instrumental composers — German and otherwise — had little room for humour. They took themselves far too seriously, especially those steeped in romantic literature. Schumann comes to mind, and Liszt who referred to himself unhesitatingly as a 'genius'. Chopin's letters, too, reveal a man who regarded everything with a sense of gravity. This, apparently, extended to the particular joint of a chicken he was offered at dinner in the house of George Sand. It was not so much the joint Chopin received, as the preference manifest in the one served to George Sand's son, Maurice, that produced the irreversible break between two of the nineteenth century's luminaries.

(All this time, Rossini stayed in bed and refined his *Tournedos*.)

At this point, I will digress. Some time ago, I happened to visit Ravenna and Paris on the same trip. In the former, I viewed the famous mosaics with their themes taken from the Bible. Visitors are not drawn to Ravenna by famous names, merely by the fine execution of scenes which have universal appeal. In Paris, I detected for the first time a curious message by Cézanne in a painting called '*Les accessoires de Cézanne*'. The depiction of a desk with an inkwell, a statuette of Napoleon, a piece of fruit, seems to signal: 'these objects are important to me, therefore they shall be important to you'.

I have always wondered if art, at its greatest, needs to combine universal appeal of the subject with uniqueness of the message. Such perfect balance was absent both in the mosaics of Ravenna, and in the particular painting which resides at the Jeu de Paume.

The reason for the digression is to suggest a movement from the predominantly universal to the perfectly balanced, to the predominantly unique. The nineteenth-century emphasis on the unique resulted in art's preoccupation with the self to a degree which, as we now realise, proved destructive. In its preoccupation to be unique, it has in fact degenerated into the worst kind of uniformity. Such a preoccupation cannot tolerate humour. Such a preoccupation, sooner or later, leads to sentimentality. Generically, it is a German preoccupation. (And now, I will get in trouble with all who reject the notion of national characteristics.)

I hasten to insert here that Schumann, and Chopin, and Liszt, and Wagner, and Brahms yield in greatness only to Bach, Mozart, or Beethoven. Greatness provides a safeguard, a shield, against sentimentality. Neither their lessers nor their followers possessed that shield. Interpreters of their music have always required exceptional strength of artistic character to escape the temptation. The road to catastrophe was long and glorious, paved with Schumann's *Carnaval*, Wagner's *Tristan und Isolde*, Brahms's *Third Symphony*. A quasi-genius of a particularly twisted mind had to appear to provide the kind of leadership which would assure us of permanent and terminal sentimentality. Arnold Schönberg obliged.

Schönberg and the demise of common sense

One wonders if it was one specific line in Wagner's *Die Meistersinger von Nürnberg* which made an indelible impression on young Arnold's mind. In Act III, Hans Sachs, real-life cobbler-poet of the sixteenth century, teaches the hero of the opera, Walther von Stolzing, to write a master-song needed to win Eva's hand. 'How do I begin according to the rules?' (*Wie fang ich nach der Regel an?*), asks Walther. 'You set the rules yourself, then follow them' (*Ihr stellt sie selbst und folgt ihr dann*), replies Sachs.

The rules Schönberg came to set at once destroyed the universal language of music invented (discovered?) by Johann Sebastian Bach, and ushered in a degree of sentimentality to surpass multi-culturalism and animal rights.

Schönberg looked at the 12 notes into which the chromatic scale is divided within an octave, and proclaimed that hearing any one of them a second time before each of the notes had made an appearance in the first place would violate the concept of aesthetic equality. (In other words, he established government of the notes by the notes for the notes.)

Schönberg found the previous regime by tonality to have been unfair, oppressive, and exploitive of the weaker frequencies. By what right did *C Major* lay claim to blazing lights? *E flat* to festive magnificence? Was it justice to permit bucolic happiness to *G*? More importantly, was *B Minor* forever condemned to despair? And how could *A* be carefree right next to *A flat*'s solemnity? How was *F sharp* to develop self-esteem?

Fortunately for the oppressed, the corresponding theory was a dead give-away. Next to the 'Tonic' (signifying the home base for the tonality), the fifth above the Tonic was called 'Dominant'. Predictably, there were entire groups of chords languishing as '*Sub*dominants'. And, although the constant alternation of the preceding was camouflaged as 'tension—release', anyone familiar with Marx's *Communist Manifesto* would know that 'All history hitherto is the history of class warfare', in which the weaker classes lose. Well, Schönberg certainly put an end to all that. In his music, the notes participate equally in the distribution of the finite supply of ink at his disposal.

How a proposition this vile both from a musical and from an intellectual point of view could have been taken up seriously, even fervently, is for scholars of the twenty-first century to sort out, right after they explain how Marxism conquered our universities. The fact is that no one has been able to put Humpty-Dumpty together again, and the dissolution of music thus preceded the dissolution of morality, vocabulary, and other stabilisers of our lives.

From self-pity to Socialist Realism
However, before opponents of national characteristics consider forgiving me, I must provide additional explanation for the earlier

reference to sentimentality as a German preoccupation. I am unlikely to be alone in noting a strong connection between self-pity and sentimentality. The first instance of self-pity on an historical scale — national self-pity we might call it — could well be the aftermath of the Thirty Years War. Although concluded in 1648, the reverberations are still with us. Germans (there was no Germany as such at the time) have never recovered from their sense of victimhood caused by the perception that a long and vicious war had been fought on their territory, at their expense, with no German interest at stake.

For some time, scholars have contradicted such interpretations, but the sentiment prevails. And long ago, sentiment turned into sentimentality in search of a national identity. 'What is German?' asks Wagner in a lengthy essay by that title, as late as 1865. It would be difficult to argue that, even in 1997, the question can be answered satisfactorily.

But Germany was to receive assistance. Perhaps it was the comradery which had evolved between the rulers of Russia and Prussia during the centuries they played with Poland, shoving it back and forth on her castors — in any event, the Russians came through. They infused politics, ethics, and all the art forms with sentimentality on a scale that was to impress a Göbbels!

They called it 'Socialist Realism' and, in its own primitive way, the music it produced managed to be more repugnant, even, than Schönberg's contorted world of the 'Twelve-tone'. Two examples stand out in memory. Shostakovitch, having offended The Party (ie, Stalin), having been appropriately punished, and having redeemed himself through self-criticism, decided to submit a peace offering to the great leader. He called it 'The Song of the Forest'. It set Stalin's reforestation plan to music with tenor and bass soloists, chorus and orchestra. A children's choir dressed as Soviet pioneers brought up the rear (and tears to party-members' eyes).

The other piece that comes to mind was an opera by Meitus, called 'The Young Guard'. It tells the story of young Russians who offer resistance to German occupying troops during World War II. They are captured, tortured and, eventually, executed. Before the final tragedy, they spend time in a jail cell at the feet of the local Party Secretary who sings to them about the dawn of the great Soviet future, certain to arrive after they had gone. Even as we sat in Budapest's Opera House, surrounded by the great Soviet future which had already destroyed the production of food and other consumer goods, and killed, imprisoned or interned all who did not submit, the overflowing sentimentality of the total experience rendered the third-rate music acceptable.

Many years later, now in London, I attended the world premiere of a Requiem by a London-based composer. Since I arrived too late to study the programme notes, I simply took my seat in the Royal Festival Hall and listened. When it was over, my state of mind was no different from the moment I had taken my seat. All that happened, I thought, was the passage of some time during which an orchestra played and people sang.

As I waited at the cloakroom, a former student of mine suddenly materialized out of the crowd. Her face was bathed in tears. She grabbed my hand in a silent gesture. Able to speak at last, she sobbed: 'Now I know how the people at Auschwitz felt'.

Unlike myself, she read the programme notes.

Invasion of 'original' instruments

In the performance of music, sentimentality produced the obsession with so-called old instruments. There is now an entire industry manufacturing (!), and an army of players using them. Before I incur the wrath of yet another constituency, I hasten to say that, as an occasional excursion into the past, people may find genuine pleasure in the playing of, and in the listening to original instruments, and in trying to piece together from scant sources what performance practices might have been in a by-gone age.

But instruments continued to develop only so long as they were not good enough. In other words, there is nothing 'superior' about so-called period instruments, or they would have remained in use. Indeed, instruments ceased to change the moment they were as good as they could be. For the violin, this occurred in the early seventeenth, for the flute in the mid-nineteenth, for the piano at the very beginning of the twentieth century. Just as composers were content as soon as the writing down of music reached its optimum form, instruments, too, were left alone once they could do the job.

The cult of old instruments to be played in modern halls, to which listeners arrive from their air-conditioned or centrally-heated, electrically-lit homes in their latest automobiles, is odd enough. Even more curious is the spectacle of orchestral players who arrive from the same places in the identical manner, and who negotiate through unions. As for pianists who insist on playing Beethoven's sonatas on a

Hammerklavier, they ignore the obvious. Beethoven went far beyond the limits of his piano — in fact, it is fair to say that Beethoven knowingly composed for a pianoforte-of-the-future already in his so-called middle period, when (for example) the *Appassionata* was written.

Period instruments cannot be properly tuned, even individually — let alone to the benefit of *ensemble* playing. So why the sweat and blood, trying to accomplish the impossible? Because people have come to take themselves very, very seriously. They actually believe that they are (and ought to be) offering 'faithful' performances in a style neither they nor their audience can possibly evaluate. In place of great performances — which come exclusively from great performers and leave no one present in doubt — we now have 'authentic' ones.

As if to furnish final proof, you cannot joke with devotees about period instruments. In fact, you cannot joke about anything at all. The last flicker of humour went out with Puccini's *Gianni Schicchi* (no, I haven't forgotten Richard Strauss) and, before that, the memorial to humour in music was erected by Giuseppe Verdi — both Italian by coincidence? While Richard Wagner built his last monument as a bridge to sentimentality called *Parsifal*, the 80-year-old Verdi composed *Falstaff*. Some credit goes to Shakespeare, and to Arrigo Boito who produced a fabulous libretto from *King Henry IV, Part II* and *The Merry Wives of Windsor*.

The 'right to self-expression' turns out the lights

But, after the total fiasco of his one early comic opera, and the great personal tragedies of his life, it was Verdi who lit up the sunset of the nineteenth century with the effervescent humour which springs alone from wisdom and kindness. At the end of three acts that, in the words of Caliban, 'give delight, and hurt not', Verdi plays the joke of the century on music's 'serious' commentators. Having endured over five decades the 'slings and arrows' of his critics who claimed that he was incapable of anything but trite melodies with crude accompaniments, he rolls out a multi-layered four-part fugue the like of which no one had heard this side of Beethoven. 'The whole world is but a joke', the text assures us.

That was then. Today, we are concerned with everyone's right to self-expression. That, one might argue, is the ultimate in sentimentality.

9

Self-indulgence, childishness and puritanism

the sentimentalisation of civilised eating

Digby Anderson

The puritanical family meal is a dreary affair

It is one o'clock. The lunch table is set for four, James Robinson, his wife Mary and their two boys, Neil and John, aged 10 and 12. They all come to the table after washing their individual hands in the bathroom. Immediately, Mrs Robinson brings in four plates. On each are two lamb chops, some boiled potatoes and some boiled cabbage. The lamb chops are over-cooked and dry. Mrs Robinson buys only one sort of potato regardless of whether they are to be boiled, fried, roasted or baked. Today, boiled, they have collapsed. The cabbage has also been over-cooked and inadequately strained. It is leaking pale green water which is seeping under the potato threatening to turn the gentle collapse into an avalanche.

In a light blue 'boat' which matches the plates, is half a pint of gravy made with gravy browning from a packet. Each Robinson pours some over his plate adding to the unpleasant mess already there. James looks sternly at the boys to see they do not take too much gravy. They try to take as much as possible to add a little taste to the dish and cover up the taste of cabbage which they don't much like. For the same reason they would like to shake on lots of pepper and salt. But his gaze deters them from anything more than the slightest try at the Bakelite pepper pot which yields scarcely anything. The pepper is finely ground white pepper and has been in the pot a long time. During its stay there it has repeatedly had to endure close proximity to plates of steaming cabbage and potatoes — they are served at least five times a week — and its tiny holes are blocked. Neil knows a good bang on the table would dislodge the accumulated damp pepper from the holes but he dare not try. The salt may not be shaken over the food — that is vulgar. It has to be poured (its single hole is bigger so it does still pour) into a little pile on the side of the plate. This is a finely judged operation. Salt adds taste so the boys want a lot. But they know that no trace of the pile must be left at the end of the course as that would be 'waste' and wasting food, indeed wasting anything, is wrong.

To complement all this, each diner has a glass which he three-quarters fills from a matching jug of lukewarm tap water. To take less would be pretentious. To take more would risk spillage. The boys would like to leave the fat from their chops but, as with the salt, nothing may be left. Indeed that is even true of the water. Glasses though not the jug must be drained by the end of the meal.

When everything is finished and only then, when knife and fork are parked correctly side by side, then the second and final course will be brought on. This is a sponge pudding made with too much flour, too few eggs and too little butter. The sole relief — doing for it what the gravy did for the cabbage — is some very sweet runny jam served in the pair of the gravy boat and subject to the same stern rules of quantity.

During lunch, Mr Robinson listens to the news headlines on the wireless, during which no one may talk. Later the weather is briefly discussed. The nearest to controversy is a brief exchange about the boys' progress with their school holiday assignment. Enquiries are made about where they are going in the afternoon and orders issued about the time of their return. When the conversation ebbs, there is silence. When the second course is finished, Mr Robinson nods to his wife, thanks her for a lovely lunch and all get up or, as they call it 'down', from the table together. Mr Robinson takes exactly 15 minutes nap before returning to work in the shop. The boys help their mother to wash up, a procedure governed by almost as many rules — plates before cutlery, change of water for the glasses, no stacking of pudding plates on first course plates for conveyance to the sink. Even the plug hole is supervised; Mrs Robinson swirls the escaping water around it so that it does not emit a rude gurgle.

In cooking, effort without inventiveness makes for poor fare

This sort of table was typical of middle income groups in Britain in the 1950s. In the 1930s things would have been much the same, though without the contributory cultural effect of post-war food rationing. It continues in a somewhat weaker form in many homes today. If we wanted a word to characterise it, that word might be 'Puritanical'. The central feature is the absence of pleasure seeking. Indeed, the Robinsons ruthlessly patrol the table to scotch any sign of enjoyment. It also follows rules and habits. Mrs Robinson does not cook what she wants, likes or chooses. She cooks what other Mrs Robinsons cook, and her family eat like other Robinson families. They do not eat what they like but what they are given and they behave at the table in the way 'people like us' behave. Feelings have no place at the table, still less feelings about food. Nor does expression, still less self-expression about food. It is not a proper topic of interest or opinion. Each person is served the same food and in more or less the same amounts. Self and individual difference have no place.

This does not mean no effort is made. Effort may not be made at expression or in taste, still less in inventiveness or refinement on the part of cook or diner. But Mrs Robinson, while not working to create a pleasurable lunch in that sense, does do her chores. She shops every day. She peels her potatoes, washes the cabbage scrupulously and watches the cooking of the meat and vegetables to ensure they are all over together. She does what is necessary. Her family, too, come together on time, eat together and in the same way, talk together and follow the rules.

The Robinsons are puritanical, provincial and insular, and proud of it. But they are not a puritanical enclosed sect. They know not everyone eats as they do. They are aware of people below them on the social scale who take no trouble with their food or manners. They know of others, some above them on the social scale, who 'should know better', who indulge themselves in food. These people, in Mrs Robinson's phrase, 'live to eat rather than eat to live' and that is obviously perverse. They give in to their appetites. They waste food. They eat according to individual taste. Worst of all, they 'make a thing about food'. They talk about it. The Robinsons don't distinguish among these people very much. Understandably, the important thing for the Robinsons is what these other people are, collectively, not like; they are not like 'us', like 'ordinary, decent people'. However, we who are interested in sentimentality must make some distinctions. The Robinsons are pretty unsentimental about food. But among the non-Robinsons, we shall find groups of eaters who are, in different ways, sentimental about food. First are the pigs.

The pigs: solitary consumption of instant food is unimaginative and antisocial

It is said of some people that they eat like pigs. Most of those who say this don't have much knowledge of pigs but, in fact, the comparison is reasonably apt. How do pigs eat? They will not eat literally anything. They do not like cauliflower or broad bean pods, cooked or raw, but they are pretty indiscriminate. Perhaps if they were given a choice of food they would have preferences, but usually they are not. Nor do they waste time eyeing up food before eating it. When they are given a pile of boiled blighted potatoes — in country parlance, 'chaps', they do not savour the aroma given off in the remaining steam. They plough in. Each pig troughs through making grunting, sloshing noises, but with no regard to the other pigs. There is little actual violence but a fair amount of jostling, certainly no table conversation. They start eating together and finish more or less together. This is not because they synchronise their consumption for sociable reasons, but because the Almighty has given them similar appetites and, since they eat as fast as possible, they finish together. When small, there may be an exception to this, a 'runt' of the litter who either gets excluded or who for reasons of his own hangs about unable to decide or work up enough energy and enthusiasm to join his siblings at the trough.

There are families in Britain and America with members, more frequently among the young, who eat more or less like pigs. The single most noticeable difference is that they have considerable choice and do have preferences, although whims might be a better term. Each human pig decides for himself when he is hungry and fixes himself something. It might be straight from the fridge and eaten with the door still open while he grumpily surveys the other contents to see if anything else takes his fancy. If he is feeling energetic, it might be a packet taken from the deep freeze and heated in the microwave. Young Pig makes no effort in preparation of his food and his mother makes little either, beyond restocking the fridge and freezer equivalents of the trough. There is no serious work involved such as Mrs Robinson does in her cooking. Not even any washing up beyond the spoon left covered with strawberry yoghurt and the wrapper from the packet left on the fridge top.

Young Pig eats on his own and therefore with no notice of others, as quickly as possible, usually standing up or moving about. Indeed, there is no possibility of him talking because his mouth is crammed full until satiation is reached. Sometimes it is overfilled and butts and gobbets drop down his sweater. Satiation may be reached before the packet or portion is exhausted. This frequently occurs because he makes no effort to gauge appetite or select the portion or packet size to fit it. When this happens, the two slices of bread encasing the microwaved sausage and exuding excess ketchup are simply left, half chewed, on the magazine he was flicking through when he started eating. Young Pig's eating is centred on self, mostly on his feelings, appetites and whims. There is little restraint or order by sociability, prudence, tradition, thoughtfulness. It is not entirely self-obsessed; he tends to select packets according to peer fashion. But if sentimentality is sentiment unchecked by reason, morality and sociability, then Young Pig's eating should be characterised as sentimental.

Food cranks are environmental sentimentalists

It is not, however, as sentimental as his girlfriend, Kelly's. Her eating is just as self-centred as his but it has the added distinction of posing as high-minded. Kelly will eat only what she calls 'natural food'. She will not eat white bread or modern farmed vegetables. No matter that the bread she does eat and imagines so brown and natural is produced by the same unnatural processes as white bread. No matter that some of it is white stained brown. No matter that the genetically modified tomato purée she rejects for her stodgy brown pasta has much in common with the organic tomatoes she fills her sandwiches with. Both are unnatural. The tomato is not natural to England or even Europe. It is the fruit of colonial exploitation. Indeed, if England had been left natural then it would still be covered with forests and not growing anything much at all. The parkland and grasslands Kelly likes to walk on are also the result of man's unnatural rearing and grazing of sheep. Kelly does not eat lamb or any other meat. That's not entirely true. She will eat chicken, including unnatural chicken, if it does not look like chicken. If it is off the bone — the bone reminds her that it was an animal — and covered with an unnatural sauce so the meat is not visible, then she will tuck in.

One strain in Kelly's absurd posturing about food is what we might call environmental sentimentality, an unthought-out, feelings-led belief in the existence of two worlds, one good and natural, one bad and developed. Another is animal sentimentality. Kelly knows nothing about the country or animals but is happy to sound off. Yet another is health sentimentalism. Kelly, who is very healthy thanks to the wealth creation of unnatural industry and technology and the advances of unnatural medicine, is obsessed with herself and most of all with her health. She does not eat like her boyfriend for instant, if superficial, pleasure in food. She does not see food when she looks at her plate. She sees potential threats to her longevity, intimations of obesity and a conspiracy by the food companies to murder her with a heart attack. There she sits, bobbing her dyed curls in indignation at the evils of additives, her little face caked with unnatural make up, her feet squeezed into tight, unhealthy shoes made from dead animals, her tummy rattling with unnatural contraceptive pills, using her lunch, her food as an excuse to draw attention to herself, more specifically her compassion for animals and her concern for the planet.

It is said that the number of Kellies has grown considerably. That is true in that there are many more people affecting concerns and calling themselves vegetarians. But food sentimentality is not new. Not only does recent history have food cranks such as the vegetarian Hitler and George Bernard Shaw's obsession with meat eaters' excreta, but posturising about food has long been associated with quasi-religious quackery from the early heretical sects to such nonsense as the 1890s Fellowship of the New Life for 'atheists, spiritualists, individualists,…communists, anarchists, vegetarians, anti-vivisectionists and anti-vaccinationists'. What is more interesting is how these sentimental ideologies can provide a cloak for a rather different personal sentimentality.

It is commonplace that many children do not like certain foods. Some do not like certain tastes. Some try to resist foods even before tasting them on the grounds of smell, shape or texture. In sensible societies, and not only those of the puritanical Robinsons, it was part of growing up to learn to eat everything and to get over such childish resistance. In civilised societies there was then a second educative process in learning to enjoy choice foods and refine tastes. Often it was precisely the once unappetising foods which later provided so much enjoyment. That is true of the acquisition of a dry palate for claret or Fino, a bitter palate for olives, a delight in the slimy oyster or the smelly, high hung hare.

Squeamishness in choice of foods is sentimental and effete
Partly as a result of sentimental, child-indulgent theories of education which have seeped from state schools into the home and been propagated by progressive psychologists of child-rearing, many parents now, far from stamping out childish phobias and aversions, allow their offspring to keep them. The result is a generation of Peter Pans at the table; 40-year-olds who bleat like tots; the otherwise intelligent, successful businessman who wilts when offered a jellied eel, 'Oooh, I

couldn't, I'm sorry, I just couldn't'. It's instructive that 'couldn't' because, of course, they have never tried. What they mean is they 'won't'. There they sit, faced with a fine dish of liver in sherry, or herring roes in butter, or calves brains, or crabs legs, or tripe in tomato with chick peas, or duck eggs, all fine foods which better men than they have found to be good, perfected and handed down in culinary tradition, and all they can do is whine, 'I'm sorry, I couldn't'. This is full-blown sentimentality, adults indulging feelings, self-centred feelings, unrestrained by self-discipline, tradition, sociability, reason or shame.

This childish food rejectionism is not new. It is especially a feature of Anglo-Saxon countries with Britain and America notorious examples. But in the past at least the Peter Pans felt slightly awkward. Today the fashionable ideologues of animal, health and environmental sentimentalism allow them to hide their personal failure; more to turn it into a source of pride and superiority. Now offered high game, Peter Pan can say, 'Actually I don't eat meat. It's partly a matter of health and partly, well, I think we all realise a little more about man's responsibility to our sensate animal friends...' As upper-class Marxists used ideology to indulge feelings of guilt, so food faddists use healthism and environmentalism to transform their stunted growth in food taste into a platform of superiority.

None of this is to suggest that there cannot be principled reasons for rejecting classes of foods. There obviously can. And among them are ones which, far from being new and fashionable, are old and highly respectable, notably those mandated by religions. These as matters of obedience are the opposite of sentimentality. In theory too, the new ideologues might be able to justify rejection. In practice they seldom do so, being intellectually incoherent and dripping with self-indulgent feeling.

Food sentimentality: wasteful of resources

Food sentimentality is not harmless. Its most obvious result is waste. There is no scientifically established measurement of the amount of food wasted in Britain. Waste occurs in several stages of the food cycle. There is waste by incompetent shops who are left with more food than they can sell and liable to become stale and degraded. There is waste in the domestic kitchen when food is bought in the wrong quantities or stored poorly so as not to be ready in the right state when needed. There is waste in preparation and cooking, and waste on the side of the plate. There are estimates that the amount of food that goes out of the back door and into the dustbin is as much as a third of what comes in the front door.

Until very recently the dominant concern about food in the world has been its scarcity. All the knowledge and value systems of the different countries are full of concerns about getting enough food. The most basic moral response which should flow from such traditions to today's plenty is, in one word, gratitude. The gratitude is not only for the bounty of nature. Nature is no more or less bountiful now than she was in the famines of the middle ages and the malnutrition of the nineteenth century. The gratitude should be for man's ingenuity in transforming nature through plant refinement, animal breeding and technology into plenty. The technology of the modern farming and food industries means that for the first time ever it is possible to feed all the world's population.

Waste is the denial of gratitude. Every time Young Pig changes his whim and leaves half the packet he has just taken from the fridge, every time Kelly turns down a steak in order to do a spot of environmental posturising, every time the Peter Pan hides the kidney in his steak and kidney pie under half his roll because he 'couldn't' eat it, they are promoting waste and being ungrateful. Such ingratitude does not hurt themselves much. But there are those whose waste and other improvident and imprudent behaviour does do damage to themselves.

The poor and food
Year by year the poverty lobby in the UK complains about the large numbers of the poor. The gist of the complaint is always the same, that there are a lot of them, that their lives are miserable, that especially their children have a miserable existence and that the state ought to hand them out some more of the taxpayers' money. But poverty can arise from inadequate income and incompetent expenditure. There is considerable evidence that many poor families do not spend efficiently. Indeed, the difference between families which manage to get out of poverty and those who remain in it has much to do with how the two groups spend money. It has to do specifically with how they manage debt, whether and how they budget, who spends — husband or wife, and how money is spent on food. The Rowntree Foundation in its 1997 report, *Small Fortunes*, found that for parents on state Income Support, 63 per cent of their child-related allowance was spent on

food. They spent nearly £22 per week, per 11-plus-year-old child on food. The lower one goes down the income scale, the more is spent, proportionately, on food. Earlier surveys show there can be considerable variation among families in what they spend on food, some getting far better value for money than others. A Health Education Authority report has complained that poor families rarely cook from raw, rely heavily on expensive convenience foods and takeaways, shop at the nearest shop and eat foods with low nutritional values. All of these practices mean the family spends more than it needs on food. None of them are problems of income or will necessarily be righted by more extravagant state handouts. They are problems of waste. Low income families also report difficulty in getting children to eat certain foods. That indicates sentimentality on the part of the children, refusing good food, or on the part of the parents unwilling to discipline them.

Good cooking involves hospitality, economy, skill and respect for tradition

The case of waste and ingratitude is but one indication that the problem is the link between preparing and eating food and morality. There is more to food than morality, of course. And the morality of cooking and eating does not have to be the sour, dull puritanism of the Robinsons. But preparing and eating food involves work, thought for others, respect for tradition, hospitality, prudence, economy and a considered view of creation and man's part in it. Trouble comes when this is forgotten as with Young Pig, and even more when it is subverted by something which poses as a sort of morality but which is not, as with Kelly's sentimentality.

The contrast and opposition between moral and sentimental attitudes to food is sharply illustrated by the way advice to women has altered over the past 150 years. Victorian advice books, and that includes nineteenth-century books in the USA, had among them many which gave advice on food, the running of the household, the duties of the wife. They are full of the language of the virtues. The wife will shop carefully, avoid waste, be hospitable, be orderly and prudent and serve others. The kitchen is not there for her self-indulgence. People more knowledgeable than she have established rules and recipes and techniques. It is her job to learn and practise them. This will involve hard work, dull repetition and a lot of nuisance. But, for instance when she cannot easily find an item in a recipe, she has to keep trying; the book gives no hint that she can improvise, let alone improvise for her own convenience.

French and Italian books are less explicitly moral. But that is because it is assumed. The great traditions in cookery, French, Chinese, Italian, Mogul, Spanish assume it involves hard work, apprenticeship and thus humility, care, economy and service. They also assume that consumption of food involves virtues, many of them the same. Thus the eater serves apprenticeship and learns taste, is appreciative of the cook's effort and, above all, is restrained.

Contrast the advice given by any of these writers on food and that given in today's women's magazines and the cookery columns of the newspapers. Modern woman is told how to cook the dish as quickly as possible so as to have more time for tennis. She is told she has no need to practise: read the recipe, then do it, this Saturday, no dummy runs, just inflict your amateurish incompetencies on your guests. She is told the main thing is to impress people with the fashionable, the new. She is allowed to substitute ingredients of her own whim for those she cannot be bothered to acquire. She is encouraged to lie and cheat, disguising this as that, to cut corners yet present things so her guests will think she has been slaving all day. Above all she is told that food is about health, or fashion, or style statement, anything other than the taste of food.

This has so far been a depressing survey. On the one hand we have the puritanical Robinsons with plenty of virtues of a sort but no pleasure. On the other, Young Pig, Kelly, Peter Pan, modern woman and the self-indulgent sentimentalists. One wouldn't want to eat with any of them. But there is a ray of sunshine. The Robinsons are wrong. Not all those who seek pleasure in food are pigs or decadents. Most obviously many who seek pleasure in food seek pleasure for other people. Even more seek pleasure with other people. Take a meal, any good meal. This one is in a private house and given by a couple for four friends. They eat pâté and then pasta with tomato and basil, then kidneys fried with onions, a salad of rocket and lettuce, a pineapple and last some Stilton and Chèvre. It is accompanied by home made bread and an ordinary Bordeaux.

This dinner involves work. The only butcher selling fresh ox kidney is a few miles away. The pâté is made by plucking and stripping down a pheasant, mincing that with pork lean, back and flair fat. There's trouble finding tomatoes with any taste to them. But more than this, things such as the bread and pâté come from practice. It's not an elaborate meal but fairly well balanced. It is economical: there's a glut of pheasants and no one uses kidney thanks to the growth in sentimentalists, so the price is low. At the same time as mincing for the pâté, the cook minces some of the pork for sausages which can then be used tomorrow when they've stiffened a little. There's more than enough and some may be left, but the cook already has thought of plans for that. The salad is from the garden — some work there too. The dressing is properly made, four to one wine vinegar and olive oil; no attempts at fashionable nonsense with exotic oils and fruit. The leaves are, as always, well dried for the dressing.

The guests come around seven, chat and drink, sit down at eight and finish at ten. There are no enunciated rules but that does not mean this dinner is not rule-governed. People eat together making sure each finishes with the other. They know what else is coming and pace their consumption — unlike pigs. They are genuinely appreciative, interested in what they are eating and grateful. The hostess is quite content to miss out on conversation and leave the table to do the pasta to order. There are more elaborate rules at work: the eaters eat as the food demands. They do not, for instance, ask for the salad with the meat. It is an enjoyable dinner. The enjoyment comes from the good taste of the food, from the sociability and from following the rules.

Good morality, mainstream Western morality is not against pleasure. Good people do not have to eat like the Robinsons. And, mercifully there are fewer Robinsons about. But it does have to be orderly and with regard for others, for tradition, work and taste. It is threatened today not by puritans but by the indulgences of the various sentimentalists.

10

All Venusians now

sentimentality in the media

Mark Steyn

Sentimentality and the 'human interest' angle
In mid-December 1995, a Republican Congress and a Democratic
White House reached an impasse over budget negotiations and the
Government of the United States 'shut down'. In practice, this meant
that 'non-essential' Federal employees — a curious designation which
seemed to cover a vast army — were required not to report to work.
For four days, America's national media struggled to report the story:
what did it mean? What was going on? Pictures of Federal offices with
nothing happening in them or of government workers sitting around
idly don't make 'good television' — as well as being, in the experience
of millions of Americans, indistinguishable from normal service at a
Federal agency. No one seemed to be affected by the 'shutdown'; it
could have gone on for months unnoticed by the majority of the public.

Civil servants cannot afford a Christmas tree
And then, on the fifth day, ABC Television finally found a way into the
story: 'The shutdown now has a human face', reported Jack Smith on
World News Tonight, America's highest-rated news broadcast. 'Joe
Skattleberry and his wife Lisa both work for the government. Both
have been furloughed. They can't afford a Christmas tree'. And
suddenly there's the story: heartless Newt Gingrich denies Mr and
Mrs Average Joe their Christmas. The crazed Republicans are trimming
not only the Federal budget, but also Joe and Lisa's tree. Congress,
like the old joke, is too mean to spend Christmas.
   As I choked back the tears, I was seized by a nagging doubt: I don't
know the Skattleberrys, and, by the time ABC had filleted them down
to a couple of nine-word soundbites, Jack Smith's report left me none

163

the wiser; but I do know the price of a Christmas tree in my corner of rural New England — five to ten dollars, according to size. Allowing for the fact that everything in the nation's capital costs more, let's figure that in Washington it's 40, or 50, or — what the heck — call it 70 bucks. In 1995, the average Federal civilian employee's income was $40,635 per annum, as against $21,696 for the average American. Joe and Lisa, being a his'n'hers Federal couple, would have a combined income of $81,270. Yet tragically, thanks to the Republican Scrooges, after four days' enforced leave, they found themselves without $70 for a Christmas tree. Possibly, like so many of us, they had a temporary cash-flow problem. As Dickens would have put it, annual income $81,270, annual expenditure $81,200, result: rockin' around the Christmas tree; annual income $81,270, annual expenditure $81,270.38, result: Jack Frost nipping at your nose.

Getting through Christmas

Across the country, there are folks drowning in debt with credit ratings at sub-zero temperatures, trying to figure out how to get through Christmas. On the other hand, you wouldn't expect to find Federal employees among them. A bank manager contemplating Joe and Lisa's combined income would surely smile favourably on a request for a $100 loan (cost of tree plus box of candy canes and a bag of Hershey's Chocolate Kisses in seasonal wrappers): for one thing, as noted above, government workers' incomes are higher than the average American's and the disparity is only increasing; between 1990 and 1994, Federal incomes rose by almost 25 per cent, average incomes by about 16 per cent; Federal employees generally have more benefits and better job security.

As I said, I don't know the Skattleberrys. I may have overestimated their income. But, if Joe and Lisa earn less than the average Federal employee, why was ABC touting them as 'typical'? Then again, it's quite possible I'm underestimating their income: in the Washington area, the average Federal salary in 1995 was $50,006 — blow 50 grand on accommodation, food, clothes, taxes and utilities, and you'll still have six over for a miniature artificial tree from K-Mart. You don't need to know the Skattleberrys to know that they're *not* average Joes and Lisas. There is no reason for Joe and Lisa to be on television at all. But, if they and their defoliated living room merit any place on screen, it certainly shouldn't be in a story assessing the impact of a five-day-old Federal Government shutdown. Indeed, you could construct a far more plausible case that having to pay for the Federal Joes and Lisas and a level of medical and dental insurance, pension plans, paid leave, subsidised commuting, child care, and alcohol and drug abuse treatment beyond the dreams of most Americans is costing more than a few struggling citizens across the great Republic *their* Christmas trees.

But that's part of the big picture, and, on the small screen, the big picture has a hard time squeezing in: you can't see the wood for the supposedly emblematic Christmas tree. Within days, CBS and NBC and all the rest had turned up their own Joes and Lisas, the 'little people' who were the real 'victims' of the Republicans' 'intransigence'. Next thing you know, Newt Gingrich the Speaker is being 'blamed' for the Federal shutdown, his approval ratings go plummeting, the Republicans' legislative programme stalls, and President Clinton's a shoo-in for re-election. It would be foolish for Bob Dole, the Republicans' Presidential candidate 11 months later, to blame his defeat entirely on the Skattleberrys, to stagger from the battlefield cursing, 'a spruce, a spruce, my kingdom for a spruce'. But their Christmas tree is a particularly sublime example of the standard media approach to important news stories.

Thoughts are being replaced by feelings

'The poet should seize the Particular', said Goethe, 'and he should, if there be anything sound in it, thus represent the Universal'. In other words, most of us find it hard to become exercised over generalities, but, if you root these great issues in specific individuals and telling details, we can relate to them: it's a principle that motors most movies, plays, novels... As the distinguished Broadway conductor Lehman Engel used to tell his classes in musical comedy construction: 'Particularisation is an essential funnel to feeling'.

Exactly. The Skattleberrys' Christmas tree is designed not to make us *think* about the Federal Government shutdown but to *feel* about it. When Bob Dole, in the Presidential debate in San Diego, kept calling for this or that subject to be taken out of politics, he was, as usual, missing the point. These days almost every subject has been taken out of politics and appropriated to the realm of feeling: health, education, the environment, gun control, drugs policy... There's no point trying to *think* about these issues; *feeling* is all. Dole's advisers told him to stop attacking teachers' unions because, after they'd run it through the polls and focus groups, it emerged that, when you attack 'teachers' unions', the audience doesn't hear the word 'unions', only 'teachers' — and 'teachers' is one of those touchy-feely things we're all supposed to be in favour of.

Sentimentality, the media and the NHS

For most of the last decade, British Conservatives had similar problems with their attempts to reform the National Health Service. If you're on *Any Questions?* or any other discussion programme, the only thing you're supposed to say about the NHS is that it's 'the envy of the world', which will guarantee you a round of applause from the studio audience. I once remarked that maybe the NHS was the envy of the odd Bhutanese yak farmer, but that I'd never met anyone in Western Europe, North America or Australia who had the slightest envy of the British health system. A week or two later, I was pleasantly surprised to receive a letter from a Bhutanese man who explained, that though not a yak farmer himself, he came from a long line of yak farming stock and that, when his parents had been taken ill while in London, both agreed that the NHS was considerably inferior to the Bhutanese health care system. It's useless, though, to venture such criticisms in public: the NHS is a rare and beautiful thing, which shouldn't be sullied by impertinent and unseemly queries about, say, the proportion of the health budget now consumed by staff salaries. In 1991, on the BBC's *Question Time*, the businesswoman Janet Cohen produced the remarkable statistic that, if things continued at the present rate, by 1995 one in every two female school-leavers would go on to jobs in the NHS. She intended this to shock the audience. Instead, they applauded: presumably they won't be satisfied until *every* school-leaver goes on to a job in the NHS. Being in favour of 'health', like 'education', makes you feel good about yourself.

Sentimental news stories are a form of emotional blackmail

In that sense, the presiding genius of the age is John Gray, author of the psychobabble mega-seller, *Men are from Mars, Women are from Venus.* You don't need to read the book — though President Clinton has apparently been through it cover-to-cover over 20 times — to figure out which is the more favourably regarded category: these are Venusian times. The 1996 Atlanta Olympics were the first Venusian Olympics, skewed to the female audience. Oh, sure, if you happened to be in the stadium at eight o'clock, you might see a beefy Uzbekistani putting the shot. But, if you switched on NBC at eight, the shot-putters would be nowhere in sight; instead, there'd be a heartwarming, pre-recorded, soft-focus biographical feature, with plenty of orchestral uplift, on a young American woman who had triumphantly overcome leukaemia to qualify for the 400m hurdles. Sports fans complained that there were no results, no hard facts; visiting athletes complained that you'd never know any other countries apart from the US were taking part. But in this, NBC's Olympic coverage was only the most spectacular subscriber to the priorities of any network news show: no hard facts, no foreigners, but plenty of soft lifestyle features that could just as easily have been recorded months ago. America's television networks were the original Venusians, to the point where virtually every in-depth investigation — on drink-driving, toxic waste, crime, housing policy, welfare — begins with a woman blinking back tears and saying, 'An' then she looked me in the eyes, an' said, "Mommy, am I going to die?"'

There seems to be no limit to the applications of this approach. Most Americans are indifferent to foreigners and their impenetrable disputes: if one group of ethnic whackoes wants to beat up another, good luck to 'em. So, in 1990, waking up to hear President Bush contemplating war with Iraq, many must have assumed it was a typing error by the White House stenographer: wasn't the designated Middle East loonytoon supposed to be Iran? But, not long afterwards, on their television screens, they saw a Kuwaiti refugee break down and sob as she told of how she'd seen Iraqi troops take babies out of the incubators in one of the Emirate's hospitals and leave them on the floor to die so they could ship the machines back to Baghdad. Dead babies: now that's good television — and as particularised a funnel to feeling as you can get.

Church burnings

In 1996, the airwaves and newspapers were filled with stories about an epidemic of black church burnings, by white racists, in the South. In fact, there are always *some* church burnings in the South — some black, some white, all very ecumenical; on closer inspection, it turned out that in 1996 there were fewer burnings than in previous years, and of the black churches burned a couple were *possibly* 'hate crimes' by white racists, but they were overwhelmingly outnumbered by the rest, variously attributed to other blacks, to local lads larking about, to bewildered crazies prematurely released from the asylum, to 'volunteer firefighter syndrome' — in which a fireman starts the blaze so he can put it out and look like a hero to his buddies — and to plain old accidents. But all that's too complicated for the news: as a result, many Americans now believe in an organised campaign of arson by white supremacists, which never happened. And once the networks had reported the story, it spread like wildfire: guilty Congregationalist and Baptist Yankees up north held collections to raise money to rebuild black churches; Jesse Jackson made incendiary speeches laying the blame for the torching of black churches on Republican extremists in Congress. Inevitably, President Clinton, a politician whose memory seems to shrink a little week by week (he has 'no recollection' of making fund-raising calls from the White House, 'no recollection' of meeting Paula Jones, 'no recollection' of being Governor of Arkansas for much of the 1980s), claimed to have 'vivid' and 'painful' memories of a racist campaign of black church burnings during his childhood — even though nobody else in that part of Arkansas remembers any such campaign. There was nothing holding the story up, but it ran and ran, apparently unaffected by the inconvenient detail that, in the real world, it did not, in fact, exist.

The news as soap opera

To borrow from the self-help shelves, life is from Mars, the media is from Venus — and, when the latter runs up against the former, it inevitably ends up adapting life to the teary plot structures it understands: the welfare mom who doesn't know what she's going to do once her benefits end; the lesbian couple doing a sterling job of raising their baby despite the wilful refusal of the town clerk and the local minister to give legal or religious sanction to their relationship; the black community leader for whom affirmative action at an American college provided a ticket out of the ghetto and who fears that the abolition of racial preferences will condemn an entire generation to guns, crack and gangsta rap...

For most people, news is something that crops up in between sitcoms, soap operas and commercials, and it is not surprising that, over the years, it should have absorbed the same techniques as its colleagues. Most news anchors are, in essence, actors playing newsmen; their sets are fake newsrooms (BBC television's is computer-generated — in other words, even the set is an act of deception); increasingly, special reports are underlaid, like any drama, with incidental, emotionally manipulative music; and, from time to time, if the story lacks exciting visuals, it's easiest just to borrow from Hollywood directly: a recent

NBC *Nightly News* story on the changing role of the CIA used clips from *The Spy Who Came In From The Cold*. Three days after the Olympic pipe bomb, CBS News was running a montage of images from the disaster concluding with the words 'To be continued...' — as if real life were no different from their moronic daytime soaps.

Sentimentality worse than sex and violence

Those who worry about the media's influence usually fret about sex and violence. Media sentimentality is a more elusive target, but it's far more pervasive, infecting almost every corner of what we now call 'the culture'. Even the sex and violence is affected by it: despite the claim that ugly, brutal television shows reflect only the grim reality of life in Thatcher's Britain, Reagan's America or wherever, when they're actually measured against reality, grim or otherwise, surprising differences emerge. According to a study by Professor David Fabianic at the University of Central Florida, 90 per cent of the murders on television are committed by whites, whereas off-screen only 40 per cent are. Blacks often complain about the lack of 'positive role models', whereas, actually, they benefit from an informal yet ubiquitous affirmative-action programme: in cop shows and detective dramas, when a black man becomes a murder suspect, it usually turns out that he is the victim of a complex if unlikely conspiracy by racist white establishment figures. Having tested successfully on *Perry Mason* and the like, this trajectory is increasingly being played out in real-life court cases. Ask O J Simpson, one of its more notable beneficiaries.

Let's not linger long over the OJ trial, whose meaning the media continue to ponder *ad infinitum*. What's revealing is the 'meaning' it didn't have: it didn't mean what murder cases have traditionally meant — that two people had been brutally killed by person or persons unknown, or known. That wasn't enough for the mainstream media, whose record on this case is far worse than that of America's supermarket tabloids and their friends in Fleet Street. *The National Enquirer*, despised in polite society, stuck doggedly to pertinent matters like the missing knife and the bloody glove — hard specifics that require journalists getting their shoes a little muddy. That's too much like hard work for the uptown boys; it's much easier to convert the story to symbolism, as *The Washington Post* and other respectable news outlets did almost from the word go, ponderously agonising over how the fall of a black role model was a tragedy for the dream of a colour-blind America. No, it wasn't. It was a tragedy for one specific woman and one specific and unfortunate friend who happened to be with her at the wrong time. Months before anyone had ever heard of OJ's opportunist attorney Johnnie Cochran, the respectable press had played the race card: even Cochran's comparison of one minor LAPD detective with Adolf Hitler doesn't seem so ridiculous, when you consider that one early *New York Times* piece on OJ managed to drag in Norman Mailer, Jean Genet, Dostoevsky, Milton, Shakespeare, and Sophocles. As *Newsweek* put it, 'Was this another case of power/money/ fame's wretched song of impenetrability?'

It's worth trying to break down the media's wretched song of impenetrability. Older art-forms — novels, say — set a premium on originality. But, in the newer media, derivative is good: audiences are more passive, so the thinking goes, and they want something familiar and comforting — not just in their fictional entertainments but also in their nominally factual ones. On the one hand, the media prefer the Skattleberrys to abstract discussion of general principles: so-called human interest. On the other, unlike novelists or playwrights, they're not really interested in them as humans: whether Skattleberrys or OJ, the complex stories of these individuals are shoe-horned into simple-minded narratives of stock characters.

In the sitcom *Archie Bunker's Place* for example, the eponymous hero, now running a bar in the New York borough of Queens, discovers the Ku Klux Klan is starting a local branch, and that all his pals have signed up; bravely, he refuses to join. Now there are all sorts of racial tensions in New York's outer boroughs — between blacks and Koreans, blacks and Jews — but the Klan is not one of them. There's more chance of King Zog of Albania showing up in Queens than the KKK.

Sentimental media stereotypes shun reality

White businessmen, by contrast, are not as lucky as blacks; they really do lack positive role models. According to the Media Research Council of Virginia, Hollywood's preferred murderer is not a drug dealer or a hoodlum but a businessman. We all know these plots backwards: the urbane property developer whose determination to build a nuclear reprocessing plant on a designated wetlands area leads him to murder; the corporate raider prepared to kill in order to get his factory takeover past the planning board... Hollywood's anti-business animus seems cheerfully unaffected by the fact that the biggest business of all in today's America is showbusiness — the entertainment industry, whose studio chiefs and rock music executives are far more ruthless than any humdrum banker or defence contractor.

We know the things Hollywood is not sentimental about. Religion, for one. Anyone in a motion picture or television drama who quotes Scripture invariably proves to be a serial killer or a child molestor. Two-parent households fare little better. Hollywood has no interest in 'family values' except in promoting 'alternative' households as their true repository: the only nuptials on America's cutest sitcom, *Friends*, have been between two lesbians; the 'issue' dramas prefer scenarios like that on *Picket Fences*, where the crusty judge rules against the reactionary gran'ma and gives custody of her grandchild to the gay father and his lover.

I can't say I blame the judge: by the end of the show, I was wishing they could adopt me, too. They were so sweet, so sober, so dignified, so responsible... and so unlike 87 per cent of the gays I know. Homosexuals, too, complain about the lack of positive role models in the media. But turn the question around: when was the last time you saw a *negative* homosexual role model? In the Robin Williams film *The Birdcage*, the stereotypical right-wing senator winds up getting lectured by the middle-aged drag queen, a Barbara Bush lookalike: 'I meant what I said about family values and the need for a return to morality.' The film preaches tolerance and understanding, yet won't permit its gay couple so much as a peck on the cheek for fear of testing that tolerance. The only mention of AIDS is in reference to the two teenage heterosexuals. Similar evasions run through *Philadelphia*, the first big-budget film to address the subject explicitly.

Sentimental treatment of homosexuality is evasive and dishonest

These mainstream entertainments are smugly self-congratulatory about their progressiveness. In fact, albeit unintentionally, they adhere wholeheartedly to that fine Christian distinction between the sinner and the sin. Even as it embraces gays, Hollywood de-sexes them: in *Philadelphia*, Tom Hanks looks good in a stick on lesion but his butter-wouldn't-melt-in-his-butt homosexuality is surely insulting to any true gay liberationist. I prefer the straightforward honesty of gay authors like Edmund White, who writes elegant paeans to the 'beauty' of anonymous sex, even the brief, nondescript, undistinguished encounter with the man who fatally infected him. I prefer that ferocious scourge of what he called 'beery heterosexuality', the late film-maker Derek Jarman, who claimed to be in a long-term 'monogamous' relationship in which he was nevertheless free to go trawling for rough trade in the bushes of Hampstead Heath every night, the ravages of AIDS notwithstanding.

I loathe homophobia — the word, that is. If you are a classicist, 'homophobia' doesn't mean 'anti-gay' but a fear (-phobia) of the same (homo-). In a literal sense, the most homophobic people of all are male homosexuals: they have an almost pathological fear of the same. Most gay men — not the ones in *Picket Fences* or *Philadelphia* but real gay men — have more sexual partners in a year than most heterosexuals have in a lifetime.

Sentimentality and homosexuality

Quentin Crisp, the octogenarian 'stately homo of England' now resident in New York, has suggested that the need for novelty is due to gay sex being somehow fundamentally unsatisfying. Certainly when Edmund White hymns the beauty of anonymous sex, you feel he's confused anal intercourse with banal intercourse. Yet, despite HIV infection rates of 50-60 per cent among the gay populations of New York and San Francisco, promiscuity isn't the issue, but the need to practice promiscuity 'safely': gay activists berate the government for not allocating funds to invent a concrete condom; gay helplines patiently explain which existing extra-strength condom works best with which oil- or water-based lubricant. But nobody seems to question what it is in gay pathology that makes this awkward, non-erotic paraphernalia necessary. Certainly, no mainstream AIDS drama does. AIDS television is *Intimate Contact* in which a robustly heterosexual Danile Massey, in his words, 'poked some dirty little tart when I was too pissed to show good judgement, and now I'm paying for it'; or *Sweet As You Are*, in which the equally heterosexual Liam Neeson did likewise with a college girl; or *Something to Live For*, in which teenage virgin Molly Ringwald has sex just once, and contracts HIV; or *The Ryan White Story* about a 13-year-old haemophiliac who receives a tainted blood transfussion; or *Littlest Victims*, about babies infected in the womb by HIV-positive mothers; or *A Place for Annie*, about another AIDS baby adopted by a loving Sissy Spacek. Even when AIDS television conceded that there might actually be one or two homosexuals with the disease, it was only so they could make television movies about repressed straights confronting their homophobia — like *Andre's Mother*, in which Sada Thompson cannot look her dying son's lover in the eyes; or *Our Sons*, in which Hugh Grant and his male lover force Julie Andrews and Ann-

Margaret to come to terms with their boys' homosexuality.

What you didn't see were dramas about gay men going into bathhouses and clubs and other pick-up joints night after night — which is how the majority of British, American and other Western victims of this plague contracted it. Even the television adaptation of Randy Shilts' *And the Band Played On*, which in book-form is unsparing on 1970s gay hedonism, found it easier to finger the Reagan Administration.

Watching television drama, you could easily believe AIDS was a disease of drunken businessmen, unfortunate virgins, haemophiliac children and perhaps the odd mongamous homosexual — in other words, just like the news and the public service announcements had said, we were all equally at risk. Crossing the highway can also be fatal — but the risk factor in crossing the New Jersey Turnpike at rush hour and a single-lane dirt road in northern Quebec is not the same. Yet there was Elizabeth Taylor, at a Wembley Stadium gala to mourn the loss to AIDS of rock star Freddie Mercury, reminding us to 'use a condom each and every time you make love'. *Every* time, Liz? So that one day the human race will be extinct and giant condoms will roam the earth, bouncing 'cross hill and dale as if in one of those amusing award-winning animated public health warnings from Scandinavia.

Sanitised media gayness sentimentalises homosexuality

America's sitcom moms of the 1950s — of *Ozzie and Harriet* and *Leave It to Beaver* — would be laughed off the screen today: the modern media like to think of themselves as more sophisticated, less hypocritical, more honest. But, in effect, they've merely transferred the protective reverence accorded to traditional households to newly fashionable groups. Even in the theatre, which can supposedly speak more honestly than television or movies, AIDS has been grossly sentimentalised, if not glamourised, to a degree no fatal illness has been for a hundred years. If nothing else, AIDS has brought about the spectacular comeback of that ancient device, the *deus ex machina* — the Angel of Death in Tony Kushner's *Angels in America*, the Hindu goddess Ganesha in Terrence McNally's *A Perfect Ganesh*. It's not enough for AIDS to be a lethal if behavioural disease; its victims have to be transformed into a vast army of conscripts engaged in an epic struggle for human dignity. As its long march through the Arts has continued, AIDS has been romantically ennobled to the point where the political and metaphorical burdens it bears can no longer be contained by the dreary naturalism of the (so to speak) straight play.

So, in the hit rock opera *Rent*, Jonathan Larson updates *La Bohème*: for, like the tubercular heroines of the last century, the person-living-with-AIDS, in defiance of his enfeebled physical condition, must be shown on stage to soar and sing with ravishing beauty. Unintentionally or otherwise, the author even offers the inverted word order beloved of opera librettists:

How can you connect in an age
Where strangers, landlords, lovers
Your own blood cells betray?

Needless to say, both *Angels in America* and *Rent* were shoo-ins for the Pulitzer.

There is something immensely irritating about santised media gayness. Yet who can doubt its effectiveness? Backed by a mainstream culture that gets a kick out of gay chic, we drift towards some sort of formal recognition of gay relationships — even though there's no indication the public is anything more than grudgingly tolerant of homosexuality; some recent polls indicate that 50 per cent of Americans think homosexual behaviour is wrong in any circumstances. In Britain, meanwhile, one of the first acts of the new Labour Government was to offer a 'free vote' on reducing the age of homosexual consent to 16. When the eponymous heroine of *Ellen* became the first lead character in a sitcom to come out of the closet, ABC Television, in its barrage of hype, helpfully provided a gay helpline number, noting that gay teenagers were more prone to suicide. Presumably, under Tony Blair, they won't be. But it might be worth comparing the numbers of closeted young gay men who have committed suicide in the last 15 years with the hundreds of thousands who have died because they've celebrated their sexuality even unto death.

Public affairs and entertainment are seamlessly intertwined
When pop culture congratulates itself on its boldness in 'examining' homosexuality or racism or abortion, what it usuallly means is that it has bestowed an approved status upon certain groups: you can 'examine' these subjects, but only in a narrow way — and heaven help anyone so unenlightened as to beg to differ. What finally did for Dan Quayle, who admittedly had had a difficult time as Vice-President, was a speech he made during the 1992 election, attacking the sitcom character Murphy Brown for having a child out of wedlock. The stampede of scornful commentators was deafening; at a stroke, the

Vice-President guaranteed the show would be festooned by industry awards, at the ceremonies for which the producers, writers and stars would earnestly declare the right of single women like Murphy to make their own lifestyle choices. In a subsequent episode, Murphy, a television anchorwoman played by Candice Bergen, went on air to respond directly to the Vice-President's criticisms. Sensitive to the suggestion that hers was an option available only to successful career women, Murphy solemnly introduced a studio-full of real-life single women from the decaying inner cities, etc, to take issue with Dan. It's worth pausing to marvel at how seamlessly public affairs and entertainment are now intertwined: a 'real' politician attacks a 'fictional' character whose 'fictional' show then uses 'real' news footage of the attack as a pretext for an attack on the 'real' politician by the 'fictional' character surrounded by dozens of 'real' people.

But the thing is, as a subsequent *Atlantic Monthly* cover put it, 'Dan Quayle was right'. The article was about whether two-parent households provide greater stability for children, something liberals still dispute. What is beyond dispute, however, is that, whether or not Dan Quayle was right about single mothers in general, he was certainly right about Murphy Brown.

Sentimentality and single parents
The next season, Murphy had her baby, a little boy called Avery, and it soon became clear that, aside from their gesture of solidarity with single moms the world over, the producers hadn't a clue what to do with him. Now that he was born, they wanted Murphy to get back to the life she'd had before she'd got pregnant. Many single women feel the same way, but it doesn't usually work out like that — feeding, nappy-changing, and so forth tend to intervene. The producers couldn't be bothered with any of that for their stellar career gal so, with the heartlessness of any crack mother tossing her unwanted kid in the dumpster, they simply got rid of the baby. Oh, sure, he's still there, back in the nursery, occasionally referred to. But he's strictly off-stage: he'd be five now, but no child actor plays him, he hasn't been seen in years; no mention is made of all the little things other mothers might talk about at the office — his first teeth, steps, words. The most talked-about television baby of the era has effectively ceased to exist. Having made him a feminist poster boy, you'd think the producers would show a measure of contrition: it seems even a wholly fictional single mom finds it hard to cope. Instead, among the media's liberal sentimentalists,

175

Dan Quayle remains an object of derision.

Media sentimentality is intolerant of dissent

That's the distinguishing feature of media sentimentality: its intolerance of any dissenting views, and the ferocity with which it squashes them. There is a kind of sentimental fascism abroad — as the Duke of Edinburgh discovered when he essayed a mild skepticism about the restrictions on gun ownership introduced in the wake of the Dunblane massacre. There are many of us who fail to see the connection between one madman and these new laws. For my own part, I think you could make the argument that, had such a lunatic attempted such wholesale slaughter at the elementary grade school in my own small northern New England town, there would have been someone nearby with his own gun who would have shot the guy dead before he'd killed more than two or three. I hope to God my theory is never tested. But it should at least be possible to discuss these things. Instead, it's one more subject ruled beyond the bounds of civilised public debate.

With most of these topics, traditional considerations such as actions and consequences are no longer relevant: it's simply about attitude. For example, in America, there is much wasteful duplication between the FBI, the DEA (Drug Enforcement Administration), the ATF (the Bureau of Alcohol, Tobacco and Firearms) and the other Federal agencies charged with fighting the 'war on drugs'. Al Gore briefly considered merging them into one streamlined DEATFBI, but decided against it because, as played in the media, it would send 'the wrong signal'. Today, sending the right signals is all that matters. Who cares if, in private, Kevin Costner is trying to build a leisure resort on Indian burial grounds? In public, he sends the right signals on Native American culture.

Sentimental media promoting feminine politics

President Clinton, a man who recently turned in an eerily plausible cameo on one of those disease-of-the-week television movies, understands. Whenever he arranges a public bill-signing, he's accompanied by beneficiaries of the legislation — the human interest, the Joe and Lisa Skattleberrys of the hour. Partial birth abortion? Here are five women, he says, who are alive today because of this procedure. Education funding? Here are five kids who will directly benefit. Expansion of NATO? Here are five soccer moms who'll soon be eligible for membership.

The Skattleberry approach is of limited use for most topics, however. With 'reproductive rights', say, all you need to know is one cold, impersonal statistic: between 25 and 30 per cent of all pregnancies in the US now end in abortion. That couldn't make it plainer: abortion is typically not an 'agonising personal decision', only a routine form of contraception. But the distraught aborter agonising publicly over her agonising personal decision sits so much better between the soaps and talk shows. Without a culture of sentimentality, it would not be possible for a civilised society to tolerate abortion. We would understand all too well what it really is.

All this slapdash sentimentality, the non-interesting human interest, the victim status for all, the empathy-junkie approach to race, guns, gays, abortion will always favour liberalism over conservatism because liberalism has a hammerlock on all the caring clichés. If men really are from Mars and women from Venus, then the Martian types have an increasingly hard time in this Venusian age. Male institutions in particular find it almost impossible to get a hearing in a feminised media. Witness the case of Lieutenant Kelly Flinn, the USAF nuclear bomber 'air ace' discharged for adultery — at least according to the fashionable commentators, whose number now includes, after an especially fatuous venture into Clintonian compassion-speak, the Republican Majority Leader, Senator Trent Lott. The more the Armed Forces tried to explain that this was a case of insubordination, of defying orders, of lying to superiors, the more the media reacted with contempt. Such archaic macho concerns as discipline, honour, integrity can no longer be accommodated in the modern media vocabulary: what counts is self-expression, being true to your sexuality and your needs as a woman — even when you're carrying nuclear weapons.

Blair and Gore

We are in for more of this, under the Blair premiership and under the forthcoming Gore Administration. Al Gore's brazenness knows no bounds. He pioneered the fashion for touting stricken relatives as the basis for public policy: in 1992, it was his son, who was nearly killed in a car crash; in 1996, it was his sister, who died of lung cancer. Gore 'loved her more than life itself', he told America in a hushed voice on live television. Then he paused. 'Tomorrow morning, a 13-year-old girl will start smoking. I love her, too.' By this time, the gaps between words were big enough to smoke half a pack of cigarettes during. 'And that is why', he continued, 'until I draw my last breath I will pour my heart and soul into the cause of protecting our children from the dangers of smoking.'

No network news anchor covering the speech saw fit to mention a speech Gore made in 1988, four years after his sister's death: 'Throughout most of my life, I've raised tobacco', he proudly told a North Carolina audience. 'I've hoed it, I've chopped it, I've shredded it, spiked it, put it in the barn, stripped it, and sold it.' No television correspondent pointed out that in 1990, six years after his sister's death, Gore was still taking campaign contributions from the tobacco industry. And why would the networks mock Gore as a fake? He speaks their language.

When a print journalist belatedly caught up with Gore and asked him why, if he was that devastated, he'd remained a tobacco farmer, the Vice-President's answer was ingenious: 'I felt the numbness that prevented me from integrating into all aspects of my life the implications of what that tragedy really meant. We are in the midst of a profound shift in the way we approach issues. I really do believe that in our politics and in our personal lives, we are seeing an effort to integrate our emotional lives in a more balanced fashion.' Nobody has mastered the feminisation of political discourse more thoroughly than Gore. Even his habit of speaking. Very. Slowly. Seems to play well with the 'soccer moms', reminding them of a concerned grade-school teacher taking the time to explain to little Johnny why eating too much candy is bad for you. Of Bob Dole's economic plan, Gore said: 'It's unconscionable. That means it's wrong, and it shouldn't happen.' Thanks, Mr Vice-President. For tomorrow's Word-of-the-day, Al Gore defines 'patronising'. In contrast to Clinton, who declares that every American child should have the right to go to college, Gore seems determined to keep the entire electorate in kindergarten.

Sentimentality substitutes style for substance

Twenty years ago, feminists coined the phrase, 'The personal is political'. They meant that the way women live their lives deserves as much attention as such traditional male pursuits as war-mongering. Today, the political is all personal, but it's not about the way women live their lives, only the way politicians live their lives — or the way they want women to think they live them. Just as Joe and Lisa Skattleberry are supposed to form our opinion of the Government shutdown, so society as a whole is meant to absorb the lessons of Al Gore's sister's death. The new sentimentalised, feminised, Venusian media-digestable politics isn't about philosophy, but style — a drag-queen travesty of what the women's movement intended.

Al Gore's on a roll now and whatever happens he's likely to be his party's next Presidential candidate — which means more human interest stories, more teary celebrities, more false empathy, and more debasement of public debate, presided over by masters of humbug in politics and media alike. Tipper must be nervously eyeing the gorgeous go-go Gore girls and wondering on whose head the next quadrennial family tragedy will fall. But as his distant kinsperson, the pop star Lesley Gore, once sang, eerily foreshadowing the new Venusian media age, 'It's my party/And I'll cry if I want to'.

11

Diana, queen of hearts
sentimentality personified and canonised

Anthony O'Hear

Undeniably mass grief

Sometimes in the history of a people there is a defining moment: a moment in which a nation discovers what it has become. In such a moment, it decides what it wants to be. It resolves what it will go on to do. Perhaps the end of the Second World War was such a moment in our history. No less certainly, in our day, was the funeral service in Westminster Abbey of Diana, Princess of Wales.

Just consider what happened in Britain on September 6th, 1997. The service itself had been preceded by scenes of mass grief and mourning no one could have predicted. It was certainly not predicted by the media. For once, those who usually lead and form public opinion could only watch and follow. The media, for all their undoubted power, could not have forced millions of people to come to London for the funeral. They could not have made tens of thousands of people queue for eight hours to sign one of the 43 condolence books or lay carpets of flowers around the royal palaces.

Misdirected but dignified grief

Nor were the people who did these things noticeably hysterical or deranged. They were, in fact, quiet, orderly and in demeanour dignified. Some of us may have felt we were in a foreign country that week, but we weren't in Iran or Israel. The crowds were British in their restraint. They were not wailing or tearing their clothes. And their emotion, it has to be said, was genuine, misdirected maybe as in the case of the man who said Diana's death meant more to him than that of his parents, and, in that sense, irrational, but it was not insincere or superficial. Whatever it was people felt, they really felt it, no matter that most of them had never even seen Diana and knew of her and her life only from the tabloids.

Mention of the tabloids brings us to her brother, Earl Spencer's speech. In many ways, this was the pivotal point of the funeral service, the encapsulation of all the pent-up feelings crying out for expression. When the Earl finished people outside the Abbey began applauding. The applause then swept inside, something unprecedented in a State funeral service, and then figuratively through the country as a whole. Few anywhere doubted the significance of what they were hearing.

The elevation of feeling, image and spontaneity over reason, reality and restraint

One of the things they heard was that Diana was a very British girl. She was, but she was a very British girl of the 1980s and 1990s. Because of her life and even more because of her death, what it is to be British has changed, irrevocably. Diana's personal canonisation, for it amounts to no less, was at the same time a canonisation of what she stood for. What she stood for was the elevation of feeling, image and spontaneity over reason, reality and restraint. The Britain of our fathers and grandfathers, the Britain of World War II has been replaced by the New Britain in which the mother of the future King publicly weeps at the funeral of a vulgar and self-publicising Italian dress designer. The pop star Elton John, her companion at that funeral, sings at her own and is later knighted for his participation in the event. And Elton John, remember, was a late addition to the service riding in on a wave of feeling which, had it existed half a century ago, would have had Vera Lynn crooning at the funeral of George VI. That such a thing would have been unthinkable in 1951 is a measure of the extent to which Britain has changed over the past 50 years.

Let us consider for a moment the relationship between Diana and the tabloids. Di was in many ways a creation of the tabloids. She was, as her brother said, hunted by them in a way most of us would have found horrific. Former government minister Alan Clark had a moral point when he said two weeks before Di's death that the press would not rest until it had brought about the death of a member of the Royal Family. (Though, sentimentality again, many of those loudest in their condemnation of the press must have been the very people who put the millions on the circulation figures of the papers when they ran Di stories.) But, if Di was used by the tabloids and the media more generally, she used them with a native cunning one has to admire.

Think of *that* picture at the Taj Mahal. Think of the 'exclusive' briefings she gave to favoured tabloid correspondents on and off the record. Think of the extraordinary interview in the leopard skin swimsuit. Think of the whole saga of the Andrew Morton book. Think of the *Panorama* interview.

Choice of the victim role

And how did Diana choose to have herself portrayed? First and foremost either as victim herself, or as one interested in victims. As a victim herself, Diana is portrayed as subject to all kinds of forces and problems, which are not so much solved as wallowed in, licensing odd and self-indulgent behaviour: her unhappy childhood; her apparently loveless marriage; her husband's unfaithfulness and supposed insensitivity; her bulimia; her reluctant divorce; her difficulties with the House of Windsor; her patronising of therapists and consulting of fortune tellers; her taking her sons on holiday with a man refused British citizenship, branded a liar by a Government investigation and, on his own admission, a purchaser of MPs' services; and the liaison with his playboy son which, tragically, ended in her death.

With much of Diana's story many women of today will all-too-readily identify. Using Diana as an example, the plea will undoubtedly be that the world be changed to fit the feelings of the victim. There is no sense that perhaps the 'victim' can or should work on her feelings to fulfil, even in the hardest of circumstances, her commitments and her duty.

The absence of duty

Her duty? In the Diana story, duty is a notion which is entirely absent, nor in the version according to Diana and the tabloids are we even to entertain the thought that Diana's obsession with her own feelings and her self-development might have done damage to the monarchy, to her marriage, to her children and, ultimately, to herself.

Diana as victim is a personification of the Rousseauian principle that the first feelings of nature are always right, and that all the restraints of civilisation, duty and commitment are harmfully repressive. In the therapeutic world in which Diana increasingly moved, one's only duty is to one's own feelings, their expression and fulfilment. If the world does not like it, too bad. You scream, you give vent to your anger, you throw yourself downstairs. This is literally infantilism, but it is part of what was being celebrated in Westminster Abbey on September 6th, and the root cause of Earl Spencer's bitterness with the Royal Family who had to put up with Diana's childlike self-centredness. You also cuddle and you confess. But what you confess is not guilt. There is no guilt and no forgiveness, because there is no fault and no God to do the forgiving. But in confessing you show your solidarity with all other victims. It is the emotional lowest common denominator, something which, as it would be said, we can all 'share'.

Her failure to understand the public role
Of course, for all the identification which countless ordinary women (and some men) will have with Diana, Diana was not an ordinary woman. She was (as we now have to say) Diana, Princess of Wales, and the mother of the future King of England. She herself was ambivalent about the role, as we see in the way she took her sons on the Fayed boat. She never really understood what it was or what it entailed. The Fayed trip was just a wonderful holiday and, from her point of view, that was all that mattered.

As a revealing symptom of Diana's lack of understanding of her public role during the finalisation of her divorce, she was reported complaining that 'I do not know any other woman in the land who has to put up with her mother-in-law calling the shots'. But, of course, her 'mother-in-law' was not just her mother-in-law. She was and is the Queen of England, and that very fact makes everything different. Not to see this, and not to see that Diana herself was not just 'any other woman in the land' is to fail to see what monarchy is all about. The fact that the majority of people in Britain think that Diana was right to put self before role and to think of the Queen as a domineering mother-in-law is indicative of the sentimentality of our time.

Perhaps it might have helped if at some stage someone had given Diana Burke to read. According to Burke, the 'barbarous' philosophy which moved the revolutionaries in France is one in which

> a king is but a man; a queen is but a woman; a woman is but an animal; and an animal not of the highest order. All homage paid to the sex in general as such, and without distinct views, is to be regarded as romance and folly. Regicide, and parricide, and sacrilege, are but fictions of superstition, corrupting jurisprudence by destroying its simplicity.

The rejection of the 'decent drapery of life'
Diana was, of course, all for the type of simplicity Burke castigates.

From Burke's point of view, though, it is sentimentality of a high degree to think that without the 'pleasing illusions' and 'decent drapery of life' embodied in the ranks and formalities and rituals and hierarchies the Dianaites inveigh against, you can have anything but a society in which the nakedness of egalitarian victimhood is confronted with the nakedness of arbitrary power.

As Burke goes on to say, in the reductionist philosophy in which a king is just a man and a queen just a woman, and a man and a woman but naked apes, all we have are 'laws supported only by their own terrors' and individuals each immured in their private spheres and private interests. Public affections — what we would nowadays call sense of community — need to be sustained by public rituals and public symbols. To the extent that in Britain the monarchy has for some centuries been the focal point of public symbol and public ritual, any move to strip away its mystery is to threaten the existence of communal feeling. Even before Diana, members of the Royal Family had started to de-mystify the monarchy, but Diana (along with Fergie) did much to consolidate and compound the process of reduction. One can, of course, argue about the ultimate desirability of republicanism. But what is sentimental is to believe that one can have key members of the Royal Family presenting themselves like characters from a soap opera, 'naturally' as it would be said, without it damaging the institution of monarchy and its symbolic nation-forging role.

Diana though was clearly not consciously a republican or a radical democrat, however much her behaviour and her attitude to formality, duty and 'stuffiness' might have had republicanism as their logical consequence. She desperately wanted her son to be king, even at her husband's expense. She certainly enjoyed the glamour of its privilege, even though she chose to enjoy herself among pop and film stars and the like rather than in the country pursuits more traditionally and more properly associated with the British Royal Family.

Wanting to be both extraordinary and ordinary

Nevertheless, her access to the jet-set life and her stardom, way above that of the common or garden super-model, though sharing something of that lifestyle, was very un-ordinary and was certainly due to who she was married to: *not* an ordinary person however much she and her supporters might portray him as such, and wish that he were. Is having your cake and eating it in this context a sign of sentimentality or just a basic confusion in which we are all implicated in trying to maintain the myth of monarchy in a modern democracy?

It is, though, in Diana's chosen role as Queen of Hearts that her and our sentimentality presents itself in its purest form. Herself a victim, she chose to speak out on behalf of victims, people suffering from AIDS and leprosy, children with all kinds of diseases and disorders, bulimics and anorexics, landmine victims, people in Bosnia and Angola. For many of the people Diana came into contact with, she was like a medieval saint: she smiled at me, and I felt better; like St Peter Claver she touched and cuddled those who repelled others, and they were saved.

Even though Diana was not Mother Teresa, there is no doubt that she did quite a lot of good both for individuals and for the causes with which she was associated. Along with all her self-indulgence and muddle, she clearly wanted to make the world a better place. She spent time and effort trying to do so. There was something touching in her reaching out to the socially excluded; it is the positive side of her sentimentality, dislike of protocol and self-absorption. Unlike the purely sentimental film star emoting over some scene of tragedy and passing on, Diana took the trouble to follow up both individuals and causes. By no means everything she did in the charitable sphere was done in public or to boost her own image. Perhaps from her point of view none of it was. People sensed this. Not all of the pro-Diana feeling was anti-establishment; much of it was genuine and positive in the way Diana herself could be.

A new form of political correctness: emotional correctness
At the same time, in her attitude to some of her causes there were certainly elements of modern sentimentality, of what might, by analogy with political correctness, be termed emotional correctness. Her choice of AIDS as one of her six favoured activities is highly significant. It is not just that it is a cause uniquely favoured by the politically correct in Hollywood and the pop world; whether we like it or not, it is a cause which has been highly politicised by its advocates. As things are in the world today, in favouring it as publicly as Diana did, one is expressing a calculated refusal to be judgmental about the activities which bring AIDS about. Diana was in fact aligning herself with non-judgmentalism about the whole gamut of private activities, and subscribing to the view that in private matters all that really matters is that we are nice to each other, and that we live and let live, no matter that some private activities do incalculable harm, not least to children.

As well as AIDS and sick children, as campaigner at the time of her death, Diana was best known for her visit to Bosnia and for her campaign against landmines. In both cases we see the sentimentality often found with well-meaning people when confronted either with evil or with intractable conflicts of interest. Of course, ethnic strife is appalling, as are the effects of landmines. But an angel is powerless against inflexible wills, particularly if one or both is an evil will, each with claims of right and tradition. There are occasions where placing landmines may be the lesser evil. It is sentimental to avoid the roots of a problem, and it is sentimental to think that there is no problem which cannot be solved with a bit of good will on both sides, and dangerously sentimental to think that reason and compassion are a match for evil. The good will may not be there and neither being smiled at by Diana nor being lectured by Tony Blair on the virtue of being modern and reasonable will be enough to produce it. For people who are themselves comfortably off, and who care about nothing beyond the present, it can be very hard to imagine how others might find something worth fighting for, even transcending good will. Sentimentality can at times make one blind to some very real and not necessarily negative human passions and loyalties. 'Caring' of the Diana mode can simply be a cover for the insensitivity of telling others that what *they* really (really really) care about is as nothing. Such 'caring' is itself a form of intellectual or emotional imperialism.

Of course both Adam Smith and de Tocqueville in their different ways foresaw that the hedonism encouraged by commercial society and the mediocrity of ambition and purpose inherent in mass democracy are not without their 'inconveniences', one of which is an inability to think of anything as being more important than comfort. Those for whom comfort and personal gratification are paramount will be unlikely to want to fight for a cause and, as de Tocqueville acknowledged, this may not be a bad thing. A certain type of oppression will be absent from a society made up of such people. But so will much else, including the seriousness which makes great art possible. Above all, such a society will suffer from a fatal inability to respond when confronted by people motivated by a different spirit. Some would see that as decadence.

The sacrificial victim canonised by popular culture and undogmatic religiosity

If so Diana, and what she stood for and what came through on

September 6th were decadent. Feeling was elevated above reason, caring above principle, personal gratification above commitment and propriety, and what Tony Blair called 'the People' over rank, tradition and history, even though without rank, tradition and history there would have been no Princess of Wales, no Earl Spencer, no Westminster Abbey, no service, no national mourning, no rediscovery in the country of a sense of community. In addition, in the days before the service, the Queen herself had been taunted by the tabloids for staying in seclusion in Balmoral, not showing grief for Diana publicly. 'Unless the Queen shows some emotion, we'll soon have a republic' we were told. She did. Charles and the Princes met the crowds and laid their flowers. The people had their service, and Britain and the Monarchy survived, but one feels, changed for ever.

What we had in that week was a potent mixture of popular culture and undogmatic religiosity, as the sacrificial victim was canonised. From all echelons of society a non-stop encounter group took over the area around Kensington Palace. The culture of caring, of niceness, of the people, was triumphant. All the tendencies described elsewhere in this book, in education, in religion, in attitudes to culture and welfare and the self, in irrationalism and in the paramount need to confess and express one's feelings, somehow came to a head that week. The crowds and their attitudes and their grieving and their clapping did not suddenly come from nowhere. But until then they had never received their full expression and legitimation. Post-Diana, Britain will indeed be another country. That week we witnessed a defining moment in our history.

12

The corruption of Christianity
the history and origins of sentimentality

Lucy Sullivan

Sentimentality makes egalitarianism mean not equal opportunity but equal outcome

Sentimentality has a history. It began in the wake of the Romantic Movement which exalted the importance of feelings for their own sake instead of for their objects and results. So, for instance, one's feelings of sympathy or compassion were an exquisite personal indulgence rather than an expression of moral attitudes which accomplished some good consequences in the external world.

Sentimentality is a major component in present day conceptions of social justice. We can trace the descent of the doctrine of social justice from its philosophical origins in the ethical teaching of Jesus, through mutations in Enlightenment Humanism and Romanticism, to its present condition in today's culture of the Welfare State.

Western culture is fundamentally Christian, its institutions and its practices founded on specifically Christian ethical premises. Most of the most prized Western social and moral values appear as explicit injunctions in the New Testament. The Sermon on the Mount insists on the equal social worth of the weak and suffering with the powerful and successful, while the Parable of the Good Samaritan insists on the brotherhood of man, asserting that we are not to confine our care and moral solicitude to those who are related to us by bonds of family, tribe, nation and race. Despite their ostensible rejection, and sometimes even caricature and ridicule of Christianity, Enlightenment philosophers drew on these Christian principles in their construction of the secular ethic of political equality and the brotherhood of man.

Christ's injunction to love one's enemy complements the equally important Christian ethic of forgiveness — seventy times seven. Social determinism likewise implies endless forgiveness, since one cannot in conscience blame the victim of circumstances. Christian forgiveness is predicated on repentance, and takes its meaning from a belief in the reality of sin, or wrong-doing, defined ultimately as a failure of dutiful love, as expressed in one's actions towards one's fellow men and women. Social determinism, however, implies that there is no personal wrong-doing in such failure, and hence no place for guilt or repentance; equally, there can be no grounds for punishment, for sanctions against, or even for disapproval, of 'crime', or for any of the large canvas of selfish, self-interested, and self-indulgent behaviour which falls outside the scope of the law. Sympathy no longer lies with the victims of such behaviour. A splendid, pithy joke of recent years is a commentary on this state of moral affairs. It is a re-telling of the *Parable of the Good Samaritan*, with two social workers in his role. They observe the man 'who fell among thieves' lying by the roadside, and as they pass on one says to the other, 'The person who did that certainly needs help'.

What is considered ultimately beneficial should, of course, determine moral principles of behaviour. The consensus on this has scarcely been challenged in the post-Christian era, and entirely reflects Christian values, despite recurring movements against Christianity, which claim precedence as providing a better route to a goal which was initially defined by Christianity. Genocide, retribution, slavery, civil violence, all ethically correct before Christianity's emergence, have never been convincingly substituted for its defining principles of peace and goodwill towards men.

The classical world exalted justice but Christianity offers the prospect of forgiveness

In the Greek tragedy *Medea*, Euripides presents an ethical problem for which he has no solution. Medea is driven to a tragic action not simply in revenge against her husband, Jason, who is divorcing her in order to improve his career prospects through a politically advantageous marriage to a younger woman. Her actions are determined also by the obligations of justice. Jason plans to wrong and hurt her, and so should be hurt and wronged in return. In the situation in which she finds herself, the only way of achieving the requisite justice is for her to kill their two sons. This exercise of justice will hurt her as much as, more, than it hurts Jason, and it robs two children of their lives — but, viewed from within the structure of

Ancient Greek ethics, it is morally correct. Medea is admirable for her courage in carrying out the demands of justice, even at cost to herself. Through the chorus, Euripides instructs us to be appalled at this outcome of the workings of moral rectitude, but he provides no solution for what might be viewed as morality failing to perform its function of ordering human behaviour for social good.

Pericles' famous funeral oration in recognition of the first Athenians to fall in the Peloponnesian War, as recounted by Thucydides, makes great claims for the moral uniqueness of Athens: it is a democratic, tolerant, liberal, free society, superior in all these respects to the other Greek states. But read on, and it becomes impossible for a twentieth-century Westerner to reconcile these claims with the genocide which follows every Athenian victory. The rational beauty of neither the Mytilenian Debate, nor of the more famous Melian Dialogue, in which communities argue for their lives, is able to prevent their slaughter and destruction.

Into this harsh world came Christianity, providing a solution to Medea's problem and a very different angle on Athens' virtue. By making a virtue of forgiveness, it would have allowed Medea to spare her boys and her feelings for them, while acting with ethical correctness. And through the universalising of moral obligation, it has created our disapprobation of the Athenian's easy genocide which to us, though obviously not to them, sits so ill with, is so contradictory of, the values of the open society applauded by both Pericles and, centuries later, Popper.

This brilliant Christian solution created, however, a difficult disequilibrium as between the private and personal and the public and political moral modes: its application requires an understanding that, although the personal is social, it is not political; and nor is the political personal. Jesus himself expressed this necessary dimorphism in his direction to 'render to Caesar the things that are Caesar's, and to God the things that are God's'. Thus, explicitly, the moral system which he preached referred primarily to personal and private behaviour — to the relationship of man to God and of man to man as his neighbour and as God's proxy, not to man as a cog in the political process.

The dilemma of Medea is a crisis of personal behaviour, while war is a crisis of political action. Christian ethics provide a far more stable and workable programme for dealing with problems such as Medea's than they do for those of tribal, sectarian and national rivalry and coexistence. The unequivocal Quaker stance against war, which includes non-resistance to invasion and genocide, in a non-Quaker world, demonstrates the ultimate logic of applying Christian personal morality in the political sphere. Clearly, it presents problems for both individual and group well-being.

It is probably this non-applicability to the political sphere, and reiterated attempts to ignore it, that lie behind one strain of a recurring tendency to irritation and disenchantment with, or to rejection and vituperation of, Christianity, in Western writing and thought. Gellner[1] comments that the sympathies of Frazer (of *The Golden Bough*), like those of Hume and Gibbon, are obviously with the religion of classical antiquity, and not with Christianity (or the world religions). But in putting the case for the ethics of the Greeks in the political sphere, Gellner (or Frazer) does not do justice to the very real contribution of Christian ethics to the private sphere, nor to the social impact of Christianity:

> The contrast is the following: ancient religion was basically a civic cult; it inculcated virtues of living or dying for your city, a kind of ethic of social cohesion and obligation. By contrast, what replaces it is other-worldly and egotistical — it teaches men to be concerned with the salvation of their own individual souls, and not to be concerned with the world, except incidentally, at most as a kind of moral gymnasium, where they prove their worthiness for another life.

While this may be true of Eastern world religions, it is profoundly untrue of mainstream Christianity which has always had a strong social, in the sense of welfare, orientation. It should also be recognised that there is a real toughness to the private morality enjoined by Christianity when it functions in the private sphere. Loving one's neighbour politically by supporting the party of 'social justice' is a soft option compared with the demand of Christian morality that you love and forgive the person who has personally wronged or harmed you, not those who have wronged others, nor people in general, so that one is simply bathed in a general glow of gratifying emotion. It asks you to give away your own wealth, not that of others whom you deem too wealthy (or wealthier than yourself). For Medea to forgive Jason is no easy task, although it is socially, and ultimately personally, more beneficial than its alternative.

The Enlightenment restated the Christian doctrine of the equality of human souls in political terms

Christianity, in its invocation of love, resorted to the passions of personal relationships in order to supply the motivation for its moral system and its sanctions. But this resort contained, it seems likely, the seeds of a volatility which was felt as soon as Protestantism rested its faith entirely upon the strength of the pro-social emotions, construed spiritually as 'inner light', while rejecting the authority of the Catholic Church (a loss of authority compounded by the demise of the political controls of feudalism, which had previously supplemented, or even outweighed, those of the Church). Muller[2] speaks of 'a project undertaken by Erasmus and other sixteenth-century humanists to civilise society through the systematic cultivation of control over human emotions and impulses'.

Hobbes, having experienced the civil war consequent on the claims to self-determinism of Protestantism, believed that a sovereign power, whether vested in king or people, was necessary to restrain the anti-social passions of mankind. Adam Smith, also, emphasised self-control as the necessary foundation for the exercise of all the other virtues — prudence, propriety, benevolence. Self-command is an uncertain beast, and as moral subordination to the peers of both the realm and the Church became unacceptable, Smith sought succour and re-inforcement in market forces and social institutions. Clearly, untutored internal resources of the love of God and man were, in the event, not seen to be enough to save men from lives which are 'solitary, poore, nasty, brutish, and short'.

Throughout this period, the backdrop to the controlling power, whether king, social institution, or conscience, was Christian morality, sanctioned by God. Thus, whether the control of the sinful (anti-social) passions and the promotion of the virtuous (pro-social) ones was internally or externally located, the character of morality was defined by Christianity. Enlightenment political philosophy therefore, unavoidably, created a major crisis for the ratification of moral principle when, at one and the same time, it sought to make the individual autonomous and to abolish religion.

The scientific philosophers, predecessors of the Enlightenment, had bettered the Biblical explanation of the non-biological physical world; the Enlightenment's political and social philosophers thought that they could better the religious explanation of the social and moral world, of man and society. Nevertheless, as I have pointed out, the Enlightenment

197

theory of politics and man was a redecoration of Christian morality: its egalitarianism a restatement in political terms of the religious equality of the human soul (with the humble equal with the great), its brotherhood of man the social manifestation of universal love, and its conception of the innate perfection of human nature a convenient distortion of the revocability of error provided for by Christian repentance and forgiveness.

Romanticism furthered the sentimentalising of the feelings

Romanticism, a minor theme in Western culture in the Middle Ages, came into full flower as, under the influence of the Enlightenment, religion was moved aside from its central position as an intellectual force. The most prominent English Romantics — Wordsworth, Coleridge, Byron, Shelley — were non-religious, or at least remote from Christianity.

Romanticism is generally considered the child of Rousseau, although he spoke to an already willing world. Key elements in his polemic are that 'man is naturally good, and only by institutions is he made bad' (*Discourse on Inequality*); that the achievements of civilisation — science, arts, letters — create wants of which the savage is free, and are the source of evils such as war and slavery, so that the 'noble savage' compares favourably with civilised man; and that true morality is found 'in the depths of [the] heart', so that religion should be 'natural', and rules of conduct do not need exposition or authority (*The Social Contract*).

If one rejects the precepts of religion, and yet they and feeling are often in accord, then without too much initial moral disruption one can place one's trust in feeling as a source of moral guidance. Christianity emphasises the emotion of (or drive to) love; Romanticism picked up this emphasis but altered its character. While Christianity emphasises the nurturant quality of love, Romanticism developed its dimension of sexual attraction, which has the potential for disruption as well as for new harmony, and translated this volatility into the political arena, as a febrile 'fraternity' which excises social divisions. The favoured overtones of the passion of love in its Romantic preoccupation, in both personal and political relationships, are those of disruption and danger — of both sexual love and political associations which defy established norms.

There is a certain truth in the characterisation of Christian morality as a straightjacket of the emotions. It requires the suppression of the anti-social passions, while the pro-social passions perform a major service in this enterprise of suppression. Love, to a considerable extent, also defines moral obligation. Romanticism exaggerates the expressive aspects of the ethical response but turns a blind eye, as it were, to consequence. Like catharsis in the Greek conception, romantic ecstasy is a release for the spirits, but scarcely a philosophy. It urges the emotions as a sole directive of action, and while its expressions may be true of our feelings, they are definitely not a fit foundation for social policy or political programme.

To act on romantic impulse is to court destruction. The danger of the Romantic Movement, in both personal love and fraternal politics, is that it urges its adherent to act with carelessness of outcome, rather than confront good sense or duty. De Rougement,[3] in his fascinating analysis of romantic love, draws attention to its alliance with death (for example, in the legend of Tristan and Isolde). In its political aspect, the tradition of revolutionary movements which originated in the late eighteenth century, it deliberately and naively seeks the destruction of regulated society.

Shelley lived out both the personal and the political applications of Romanticism, and his poetry consistently expresses its emotional intensity, necessarily detached from sober reality. *A Dream of the Unknown* uses an extended image of the contemplation and gathering up a multitude of flowers into a nosegay, to represent the exploration, the exercise, and the fanning to a high pitch of the emotions, in what can only be a semblance of love, for it is pure internal volatility and has no object:

That I might there present it — O! to Whom?

Hymn to the Spirit of Nature relishes the glamour of Romanticism's vacuous destructiveness. Addressed to 'Life of Life!', it concludes:

And the souls of whom thou lovest
Walk upon the winds with lightness
Till they fail, as I am failing
Dizzy, lost, yet unbewailing!

The pain of the unavoidable collision of this feckless flight, post-adolescence, with the realities of life, is celebrated in *Ode to the West Wind*:

199

I fall upon the thorns of life! I bleed!
(Shelley's poetry is awash with exclamation marks.)

The greatest writers of English literature have mounted a recurring resistance to the tendency of the Christian evocation of love to spin off into Romanticism. The tradition of courtly love was one of the romantic tendency's first social manifestations. While the Court of Love established by Elinor of Aquitaine could be viewed as a useful enterprise to civilise men for the benefit of women in a barbarous age, the continental Arthurian romances have a vaporous religiosity quite removed from Christianity's concern with social welfare. The great achievement of Malory's *Morte d'Arthur* is to convert the cycle of these tales into a socially responsible form which is perhaps the first expression of the British code of sportsmanship. The latter, Guerber observed,[4] is in marked contrast to the classical Greek admiration of cheating and cunning between adversaries. With engaging charm, Malory develops a code which both allows for masculine pugnacity and competitiveness (which romantic revolutionarism also serves), and binds it to the cause of social order. A failure to observe this code by Gawain and his brothers eventually destroys the whole Arthurian society.

Shakespeare, too, takes issue with the courtly heritage, most directly in his criticisms of the non-empiricism and absurdity of the courtly language of love, in the Sonnets and in Rosalind's mockery in *As You Like It*. *Romeo and Juliet*, far from being a paean to romantic love, is a demonstration of the harm caused to the young by the encouragement of over-blown and unrealistic sexual emotion. The fanciful nature, and changeableness of young affections is clearly stated via Romeo's first appearance besotted with a girl who is not Juliet, creating a frame for the death of the two for 'love' as an absurd waste, culturally engineered.

Jane Austen's writing is contemporary with the advent of the Romantic Movement, and she sets herself against it. *Northanger Abbey* is a fairly light-hearted, and to that extent superficial, mockery of the labouring to produce situations worthy of romantic sentiment which the Gothic novels of the period represent. *Sense and Sensibility* presents a serious opposition to the ethical favouring of emotion which Romanticism embodies, closely argued by means of the novel's demonstrative apparatus, plot. The lines of division, and Austen's moral preference, are laid down at the outset in the character delineations of the sisters, Elinor and Marianne:

Elinor "had an excellent heart; her disposition was affectionate, and her feelings were strong: but she knew how to govern them…"

Marianne "was sensible, clever, but eager in everything; her sorrows, her joys, could have no moderation". The knowledge of how to govern her feelings, she "had resolved never to be taught".

Then Austen declares that romantic feeling, or sensibility, owes little to disposition. It is neither a sign of inordinately strong feelings, nor of the absence of mental powers. It is, in effect, an ethical choice. Marianne considers her aptitude for unrestrained emotion to be a sign of moral superiority, and in response to Elinor's cautious and reticent expression of her love for Edward, retorts: 'Esteem him! Like him! … Use those words again, and I will leave the room this moment' — as if in response to an indecent act.

The working out of the novel, in which the two sisters form attachments to young men with concealed impediments to their marriage, demonstrates the happy resolution for the couple who temper emotion with prudence and propriety, and the perhaps unnecessary frustration of the pair who pride themselves on their commitment to guidance by feeling.

Wordsworth began as a revolutionary Romantic, committed to the Rousseauian assertion of an innate moral perfection which is only harmed by constraint, and of the evil of the social forms which impose that constraint, but ended a 'patriotic, conservative public man'.[5]

The relatively early poem, *England and Switzerland, 1802*, is an invocation of Liberty, newly lost in Switzerland and deemed to be at risk in England. Liberty, in romantic fashion, assumes the nature of an emotion, akin to the emotional response to mountain (Switzerland) and sea (England), not a political reality, hard won and sustained by vigilance and effort. *When I have borne in memory* gives a romantic preference to revolution and seclusion above industry and trade:

> …how ennobling thoughts depart
> When men change swords for ledgers, and desert
> The student's bower for gold…

His *Ode on Intimations of Immortality from Recollections of Early Childhood* (begun in 1802) echoes the Rousseauian belief that at birth we are most entirely spiritual, and that we are progressively depraved by our contact with culture:

> Heaven lies about us in our infancy!

Shades of the prison house begin to close
Upon the growing boy

But the later *Ode to Duty* rejects the value system expressed in these early poems, and is, in effect, a recantation of Romanticism. Wordsworth declares that love and freedom are inadequate as guides to behaviour:

I, loving freedom, and untried,
No sport of every random gust,
Yet being to myself a guide,
Too blindly have reposed my trust.

Although the romantic emotions may, on occasion, appear to have served, it is only because of good luck or an unconscious deference to duty — duty, as defined by the authority of religion, being the only sure guide.

Nineteenth-century sentimentality tried to connect the emotional luxuries of Romanticism and Christianity

Romanticism with its exultation in feeling, has much in common with the sentimentality of the nineteenth century which succeeded it. But Romanticism's reckless use of emotion is very different from sentimentality's: sentimentality, while relishing emotion, is cautious. The poem, 'the lesson of the moth', in Don Marquis' *archy and mehitabel* (first published 1931) provides an exemplar of both romanticism and sentimentality. The address is to a moth hammering at an electric light globe. 'Have you no sense?' the speaker asks.

'plenty of it he answered/but at times we get tired/of using it/we get bored with the routine/and crave beauty/and excitement/fire is beautiful/and we know that if we get too close it will kill us...it is better to be a part of beauty/for one instant and then cease to/exist than to exist forever/and never be a part of beauty'

The questioner reflects: 'myself I would rather have/half the happiness and twice/the longevity/but at the same time I wish/there was something I wanted/as badly as he wanted to fry himself'

The beauty and terror of romantic sentiment, its destructive and fantastic emotional indulgence, are nicely caricatured, but have also become an object of sentimentality. The moth at the light globe (if this were a deliberate choice rather than a mistake for a candle flame) is itself an apt image of sentimentality: the indulgence of the demonstrative forms of an emotion while protected from the consequences such behaviour inflicts.

Sentimentality, in its nineteenth-century form, attempted to reconnect the emotional luxury of Romanticism with Christianity — to make into one cake the ecstasy of Romanticism and the social obligation of Christianity. That is, it would ignite the essentially restraining, though also gratifying, emotions which support Christian morality to a romantic intensity, to enjoy both the release Romanticism takes from the emotions and the safety Christianity builds on them. This was not an entirely unworthy project, perhaps being an attempt to tempt the lost sheep back to the fold with a fodder for which they had gained an appetite, at a time (the beginning of industrialism) when Christianity's moderating and solicitous influence was sorely needed. But it was a difficult, perhaps impossible, coalition to maintain, and the result inclined instead to a sickly sweetness with little moral impact.

While Romanticism, however wrong-headedly, perceived emotion as a source of guidance, sentimentality, in its full sense, simply wallows. It implies no action. Nevertheless, the burgeoning of sentimentality marks a return to the influence of Christianity in moral matters, for the nineteenth-century wallowing in sentimentality is within a strictly Christian code, in the deference it pays to the weakly members of society — the sickly, the poor, the dying, the naive — as seen, *par excellence*, in Dickens. Nineteenth-century sentimentality in literature was on occasion an instrument of social reform, as in the case of Thomas Hood's *The Song of the Shirt*, in which circumstances it almost loses its sentimental character; but more generally it created a dissociation of feeling and moral action, for it employed emotion in the romantic mode of self-pleasuring, rather than with Christianity's binding of it to the rod of personal moral initiative, or, as the nineteenth century came to call it, duty.

Dickens has been credited, perhaps rightly, with a place in the reform of some dysfunctional nineteenth-century instruments of government, particularly the law as it applied to bankruptcy, and the institutional care of children. And yet his appeal to the emotions is entirely sentimental, and the call for action is not to the emotor (or reader) but to an essentially impersonal and judicious political system. We do not need to experience the poignancy of the Chancery's prisoner's death after 20 years of futile imprisonment (*Pickwick Papers*), to understand that the processes of law he suffered under were both inhumane and ineffective in terms of their object; nor are those who relish most the waves of pity Dickens sought to elicit most likely to be those who will take personal action to achieve reform.

True, in a democracy (at that time only partially in place) the arousal of personal sentiment may flow on into the political process. But what we find in Dickens is an essential misuse of the springs of personal moral action through their importation into an impersonal political context: hence the maladaptiveness of his method, and the creation of a dangerous precedent which has revived and metastasised a century later.

There was both explicitly Christian and secular intellectual resistance to the nineteenth-century sentimentalisation of morality. Charlotte M Yonge mounted a specifically Christian defence against many nineteenth-century trends in behaviour and manners in her long novels of Victorian family life, and, like Austen, used plot to demonstrate, or provide an argument in favour of, certain styles and standards of behaviour as productive of beneficial social outcomes. In *Bywords*, Yonge (in agreement with Wordsworth) argues against the inadequacy of the warm gush of feeling and its unreasoned expression which is sentimental morality, as compared with the guidance offered by Christian precept and construction of duty. As in Austen's *Sense and Sensibility*, the protagonists are two sisters, one believing in the superiority of her natural warmth and unconsidered generosity, the other more restrained and deferential to outer as well as inner guidance, and therefore less immediately attractive to those she would serve. As in *Sense and Sensibility*, a sequence of events demonstrates the harmfulness, not in this case to self, but to others, of the more spontaneous and apparently more loving nature.

The Enlightenment philosophers and Romantics had made the concept of sin unpopular. The Victorians re-balanced the Christian equation by replacing it with 'duty' — the positive side of action whose neglect or contravention is the negative 'sin'. This re-established the cycle of error and repentance leading to forgiveness as a sanction on ethical, pro-social behaviour. The significance of duty and repentance in the cycle of error and forgiveness is roundly asserted by Carlyle in a discussion (in his lecture *The Hero as Poet*) of Dante's *Divine Comedy*. 'Repentance', he says, 'is the grand Christian act', and defines the 'one great difference' between 'Paganism and Christianity'. The chief virtue in the former is, he says, courage in the face of the vicissitudes of nature (including men), while the latter describes the 'Law of Human Duty, the Moral Law of Man'. Dostoevsky, too, constantly embattled with a current doctrine of moral vacuum if God is 'dead', asserted most notably in *Crime and Punishment*, the unavoidable experience of guilt, and the role of repentance in re-establishing humanity in the sinner.

Gilbert, in *The Pirates of Penzance*, draws together and mocks most of the elements of the Victorian sentimental development and its subjugation by the concept of duty. Major-General Stanley appeals to the pirates to pity his orphan state, so that they, taking pride in their possession of 'feeling', refrain from their normal piratical behaviour (their compassion for orphans has become so well known that it is exploited by all they encounter, making the conduct of their 'profession' almost entirely unsuccessful); further, Major-General Stanley's ploy is largely irrelevant to his object — prevention of the marriage of his Wards in Chancery to the pirates (who are orphans themselves!). Then, on the side of sentimental forgiveness, the troop of policemen, in the lyric 'A policeman's lot is not a happy one', bemoan the unfortunate nature of their duties which require the punishment of criminals who, while admittedly vicious ('the coster...jumping on his mother'), also possess some of the more amiable human qualities ('he loves to lie a-basking in the sun').

There is a long play on the possibilities of moral contradiction in the concept of duty in the conundrums of Frederick's duty to return to piracy when he finds he is not out of his indentures, to betray his future father in law to the pirates to whom he is again bound, and to abandon his betrothed, Mabel, for the same reason. Finally, in this absurd interplay of private and institutional morality, all prior commitments are relinquished 'in Queen Victoria's name', not in deference to sovereignty, but because, sentimentally, 'with all our faults, we love our Queen'.

The nineteenth-century Christian fightback, with its establishment of duty as a moral imperative beyond feeling, was so successful that sentimentality was profoundly scorned in the first half of the twentieth century. In place of sentimental effusions over conditions of vice and poverty, an entirely new arm of government was built, and social welfare, formerly the domain of the Church, was added to its concerns. This relocation of the Church's historic welfare enterprise as a department of government was a largely Christian endeavour, coincident with, rather than resulting from, the increasing democratisation of the political system, and in its initial form it sentimentalised neither poverty, incompetence, nor vice.

**In the twentieth century, romantic insouciance is supported
by the welfare state**

In the latter part of the twentieth century, beginning in the 1960s,
sentimentality (as defined above — a safe version of Romanticism)
re-emerged in Western, particularly English-speaking, societies, in
political as well as personal guise, engendered now by Marxism and
Communism, both of which had developed out of Enlightenment
political philosophy. Thus primarily, it followed on from an anti-
Christian expression of fundamentally Christian values. Although the
romantic impulse to explicit political destructiveness was an early
manifestation in this development, it came in a mannered form — a
sort of acting-up of gilded youth against the exceptionally benign (apart
from the slip-up of conscription for the Vietnam War) paternalism of
the welfare state. As the decades have progressed, the revolutionary
impulse has receded, while the sentimental egalitarian impulse, as if
directed by Gramsci, has invaded the settled workings of government,
the Church, and the educational system. An egalitarianism that could
not be sold as ideology has been sold as sentimentality.

The romantic sentimentality of the Western world's 'greening' was
manifest in the catchwords of the time — 'flower power', 'make love
not war', 'sweetness and light' — and in the hippie and environmental
movements, both of which owe a conceptual debt to Rousseau's noble
savage (and both of which rely on generous financial support from
the technological culture which they ostensibly reject). And it effectively
reviled and deconstructed the Victorian concept of duty, which had
grounded the excesses of nineteenth-century romanticism and
sentimentality.

Under the influence of post-Marxism, and its sociological
counterpart, post-structuralism, the Romantic adulation of simple or
peasant life was transferred to the working classes, the disadvantaged,
and the 'oppressed'. Wordsworth's sonnet, *Admonition to a Traveller*,
warning against the sentimentalisation of poverty:

Yea, all that now enchants thee, from the day
On which it should be touch'd would melt away!

could well have been enlisted to provide metaphorical warning against
the 1970s spectacle of the middle classes praising and embracing
supposed working-class manners and values. The result of this
denigration of middle-class models of discipline and competence, and
of welfare support for their non-observance, has been, within less than

two decades, the creation of a dependent underclass — the drug-addicted, the violent, the unemployed, the promiscuous — whose degradation, like poverty in the nineteenth century, is sentimentalised as 'real life'. In response, twentieth-century sentimentalists have demanded, and still demand, justice and reparations for the victims of their social delusions. As with nineteenth-century sentimentality, the twentieth-century application of the powerful principles of universal love and forgiveness is an unbalanced equation, resulting from an only partial implementation of Christian principles.

Jesus provided a considerable body of pointers to their practical ramifications which are in important ways at odds with current notions of 'social justice'. The *Parable of the Talents*, for example, poses severe problems for the modern sensibility's passive conception of fairness and rights, and one now feels that, to make an acceptable point, it should have been the man with the intermediate number of talents who buried them in the sand and was reprimanded as an unfaithful servant. The proponent of social justice is confident that nothing should be expected of the man with only one talent, when the others were given more, and that he should be given a share of the earnings of the men who put their talents to work, and probably that he should be allowed to bury this booty in the sand and then present it as his own accomplishment. No doubt it was specifically because of the very human tendency to demand advantages because of disadvantages, that the parable allots roles as it does: he of fewer talents needs to be told most explicitly to use what he has. To do otherwise, to say that he is excused from the common tasks of humanity, is to dehumanise and disempower him.

The parable of the talents acknowledges difference in ability or position, but does not therefore excuse the 'disadvantaged' from effort. It insists that all accept responsibility in the tasks of life. By contrast, the current, sentimental response to 'disadvantage' is to treat it as a badge of dependency. It was not a discovery of Christian teaching, nor of Marxism, that each member of society requires an adequate share of the material goods which that society produces, nor that his membership requires his participation in the enterprises of society, not just his presence. Every primitive society functions on these principles. But, post Christianity, we do, apparently, need to be reminded that love and caring do not remove the obligation for personal effort. It is not inequality as such, or disadvantage, that has created the social mess that welfare is exacerbating as it seeks to repair it, but rather the theory that inequality in talents is an unnatural condition and, worse, that it reflects on human dignity and worth.

Our present biases incline us to interpret the *Parable of the Prodigal Son* as supporting the sentimental ethic of the immorality of punishment. But this is only so if we focus on the father's joyful welcome of his son, and ignore two important elements of the story which are crucial to its religious and secular application. Firstly, the son has experienced the wages of his wrong-doing (or insouciance), and has 'lain among the swine'. He has seen the effects of his folly and his repentance is informed as well as emotional. Secondly, it is by his repentance, not by his return to ask for help, that he regains human status (places himself within the aura of his father's love); but he does not have his secular status restored to him. When the older brother complains to the father at the bounty of his welcome (killing the fatted calf), the father assures him of his respect and that 'everything I have is yours'. There is no suggestion that the prodigal can waste the things of 'Caesar' and have them returned to him as a gift. In the material sense, the prodigal son's initial inheritance has gone forever, although he may work to re-achieve a similar status; spiritually, his inheritance is always reclaimable, totally, provided he actively repents.

Current conceptions of social justice and welfare miss these important truths of the needs of human nature when they, in effect, insist that the son should now receive a share of the remaining inheritance which should have belonged entirely to the older brother. This is the version of love and forgiveness which our post-1960s welfare policies, indifferent to prodigality, have embraced. The feckless young woman who bears a child without taking thought of the realities of parenting is to be maintained in an economic position equal to that of her careful sister — and again, and again; the father of the child is to be allowed to proceed as if his action in producing this child was no responsibility of his; the couple who divorce on the pretext of 'irreparable breakdown of marriage' (which may be so minor as to permit living in the same house without sexual relations) are to be given every assistance to maintain their standards of living, and establish new families, as if their earlier prodigality had never occurred or was in no way their choice of action, their responsibility; young offenders are not to be convicted because the stigma may affect their future lives.

The prodigal son was probably hurt by the loss of his inheritance, but one assumes he also saw the justice of it. In the current moral

climate, this justice is denied, and in its place is put the sentimentalisation of the disadvantage of those who suffer the results of
their own actions. The effect is to encourage licentiousness. Someone,
and often someone besides the indolent perpetrator of prodigality,
will be hurt, and the late twentieth-century sentimentalist congratulates
himself on his loving-kindness in appreciating this hurt (while ignoring
its origins) and redistributing the fruits of the employed talents of
others in order to make it good. Unfortunately, now we are launched
in this programme, the numbers of the prodigal, and therefore of those
who will be stranded by a return to stringency, have multiplied
exponentially. As Herbert Spencer observed, 'The ultimate result of
shielding men from the effects of folly is to fill the world with fools'.
Shelley at least wanted to be admired for his self-inflicted suffering,
not pitied and helped.

For all his mushiness, Dickens did not take the step of senti
mentalising crime, even in the disadvantaged, the poor. We are not
asked to feel for or excuse his wicked or vicious characters of whom
there are plenty. This further step was largely left for social determinism
of the twentieth century to take.

Sentimentality tries to transpose into the public sphere moral imperatives which can operate only in the private sphere

The political version of the extremes of sentimental lunacy is enacted
in Simeon Simcock, the rector in John Mortimer's television series,
Paradise Postponed. Because of unresolved guilt over a long-past
adulterous love affair and its unhappy continuing product, a daughter
unloved by her mother, Simeon leaves his share of his brewing family
fortune to the now-deceased daughter's unpleasant husband, while
his own wife, so far as he is concerned, is unprovided for. Simeon's
Christianity is all political, with peace unto men transformed into CND
activism, and brotherhood into state welfarism. He, guilty in his own
terms, enjoys the benefits of his brewery family connection while he is
alive, but his penance is to deprive his wife and sons of it after his
death. He regards himself with reverence as a mystery and something
of a saint, which is his public reputation, although those closer at hand
exhibit some scepticism and a measure of amused tolerance.

Through him, Mortimer puts the case that the origin of New Left
ethicism, and what has come to be called political correctness (an
acknowledgement of Marxism as its generating force), lies in personal

or class sin. It is a public expiation, dressed up as virtue, of a private fault. But this explanation presupposes the sense of sin, of wrong-doing, which twentieth-century sentimentality has sought to erase: the eradication of guilt as an acceptable emotion and the elimination of duty, have been crusades of twentieth-century sentimentalism. Social determinism cannot, however, eradicate the guilt of the economically well-off, such as Simeon, in being what they are. As Marxism has become an intellectual- and bureaucratic-class (rather than working-class or disadvantaged-class) movement, the guilt of class can only be removed, for its adherents, by exonerating those who 'identify' with the disadvantaged, regardless of their actual levels of privilege (capitalists and conservatives, of course, remain guilty).

In Drabble's recent book, *The Witch of Exmoor*,[6] a vigorous proponent of social justice is stopped in his tracks by the prospect of a legacy to endow and establish the Just Society (in an isolated valley). He is seized by the realisation that it is an impossibility, that the whole concept is a nonsense. But the real problem for the Just Society is not, as Drabble suggests, human 'envy, greed, violence and insincerity'. The characteristic of social justice that makes the Just Society impossible is its own definition of equality and justice, which is in itself an injustice. The determination that outcome should be unrelated to input — that regardless of input in quantity and quality, each is entitled to the outcome of the greatest quantity and quality — is unjust. We all know that some of us work harder than others, that some of us are more self-indulgent in our choice of work than others, that some people do many things better than we can, and that some people do necessary things that we would not want to do. We all know that starting behind does not necessarily mean finishing behind, and that starting in front does not necessarily mean finishing in front. The false promise in social justice is that, despite personal limitations and errors, and regardless of choice and action, one can justly demand the best of all possible worlds, and not just one's just deserts.

Mistaken also is the *a priori* assumption that equality of outcome is reckoned only in material goods and status, not in the quality of self-fulfilment and satisfaction. 'Cathy and her friends', in the television documentary *Seven-Up* which follows the lives of a group of children of the 1960s, were indignant at the veiled suggestions of the interviewer that, with their working-class childhoods and lower middle-class adulthoods, they had missed out on any of the important and worthwhile things in life, and emphatic that they had not.

The bureaucratic conception of social justice bears a close family resemblance to the original principles of Christianity. Its error lies in its acceptance into the public sphere of a moral system which can only function in proper balance, with all its cogs engaged, as it were, and producing the proper output, in the private sphere. The logical consequences of action in the public sphere must be maintained if the material and economic, as opposed to the domestic and social, machinery of human culture is to function. The private sphere, also, is suffering from the excision of part of its mechanics, the recognition of wrong-doing and repentance, which parallel the public sphere's crime and punishment. Socio-economic egalitarianism, romantic goodwill, and the impeccable moral badge of social justice, divorced as they are from the realities of the human condition, are damaging sentimentalities. It is time to move on. As Tennyson said, in the words of the dying King Arthur, with all his goodly company of knights destroyed:

The old order changeth, yielding place to new,
Lest one good custom should corrupt the world.

The Fabian solution, temporarily so efficacious, has become dissolute
Sentimental policies are not benign. Produced in the name of social justice, they demoralise and manipulate people's lives. They represent a degraded egalitarianism which has come to mean not equal human worth but equal socio-economic status. Confounded by the false supposition that inequality of status and wealth owes nothing to inequality of ability and effort and everything to the working of a malevolent society, the good and useful concepts of integrity and responsibility have been almost entirely eliminated from the moral and social sphere.

Notes and references

Chapter 2

1. N Postman, *Amusing ourselves to death*, London: Methuen, 1987.
2. T Brewin, *Relating to the relatives: breaking bad news, communication and support*, Oxford: Radcliffe, 1996.
3. W James, *The varieties of religious experience*, New York: Vintage, 1990.
4. G C Williams, Addendum to T H Huxley, *Evolution and Ethics*, New Jersey: Princeton University Press, 1989.
5. R Dawkins, *The blind watchmaker*, London: Penguin, 1988.
6. M Ridley, *The origins of virtue*, London: Viking, 1996.
7. R M Nesse, G C Williams, *Why we get sick: the new science of Darwinian medicine*, New York: Times Books, 1995.
8. P Skrabanek, J McCormick, *Follies and fallacies in medicine*, Glasgow: Tarragon, 1989.
9. B G Charlton, 'Philosophy of medicine: alternative or scientific', *Journal of the Royal Society of Medicine*, 1992, 85, pp 436-438.
10. C Newman, *The evolution of medical education in the nineteenth century*, Oxford: Oxford University Press, 1957.
11. Skrabanek and McCormick, op cit.
12. J P Bunker, H S Frazier, F Mosteller, 'Improving health: measuring effects of medical care', *Millbank Quarterly*, 1994, 72, pp 225-259.
13. M Little, *Humane medicine*, Cambridge: Cambridge University Press, 1995.
14. B G Charlton, 'The moral case against psychotherapy', *Psychiatric Bulletin of the Royal College of Psychiatrists*, 1991, 15, pp 490-492.
15. M Harris, *Magic in the surgery*, London: Social Affairs Unit, 1994.
16. Ibid; Charlton, 1991, op cit.
17. R S Downie, B Charlton, *The making of a doctor: medical education in theory and practice*, Oxford: Oxford University Press, 1992.
18. B Charlton, 'Keeping your distance: manners in the surgery' in D Anderson (ed), *Gentility Recalled: 'mere' manners and the making of social order*, London: Social Affairs Unit, 1996.

19. J Willis, *The paradox of progress*, Oxford: Radcliffe, 1995.
20. Charlton, 1996, op cit.
21. Willis, op cit.
22. J Le Fanu, 'A healthy diet: fact or fashion?' in P Berger et al, *Health, lifestyle and environment: countering the panic*, London: Social Affairs Unit and New York: Manhattan Institute, 1991.
23. Nesse and Williams, op cit.

Chapter 3

1. E Voegelin, *The new science of politics: an introduction*, 1987.
2. The reader might want to compare my argument with Adorno and Horkheimer in *The didactic of the Enlightenment* (1990) as well as McIntyre's *After Virtue* (1981). For a fuller discussion of my contentions about the Enlightenment Project see N Capaldi, (forthcoming — in press) 'The Enlightenment Project in the analytic conversation' (Kluwer). Capaldi's thesis is that the Enlightenment Project is incoherent, flawed, and has collapsed. See also M Cranston, *Philosophers and pamphleteers* (1986); T Sorell, *Scientism* (19910; and J Gray, *Enlightenment's wake* (1995).
3. S Steele, 'Affirmative action must go', *New York Times*, 1 March, 1995, A15.
4. S Steele, *The content of our character*, New York: St Martin's Press, 1990, p 115.
5. E van den Haag, 'Jews and Negroes', in R Nieli (ed), *Racial preference and racial justice*, 1991, p 391.
6. N Glazer, 'Racial quotas' in ibid.
7. A thesis we cannot develop here is the notion that different religions and denominations responded differently to the Enlightenment Project and to the liberal paradigm. That is why, among other things, Catholic liberation theology is not an example of the liberal paradigm in the same way that liberal Protestantism is. Denominational positions on public policy can be illuminated by noting the response to the Enlightenment Project.

Chapter 4

1. R Scruton, *Animal rights and wrongs*, London: Demos, 1996, pp 99-103.
2. We had better leave to one side the obvious point that Scruton's stipulative definition carries the implication that what we are calling 'justified sentimentality' is not sentimentality at all, but some other legitimate thing.
3. J Austen, *Sense and Sensibility*, London: Penguin Books, 1995.
4. Stendhal, *Scarlet and Black: a chronicle of the nineteenth century*, London: Penguin Books, 1953.
5. D Marsland, *Seeds of bankruptcy*, London: Claridge, 1988.
6. In the case of British television, we also see an endless string of nonsense programmes depicting the extremely tolerant British as racists, sexists,

homophobes, etc.

7. A Koestler, *Scum of the earth*, London: Jonathan Cape, 1941, p 71.

8. The IRA, for example, are totally unmoved by the clear evidence that neither the Irish Republic nor most Northern Irish people want them in charge. Their hugely false version of the reluctant British presence — 'a military occupation' — is classic sentimentality.

9. The Germans of the Nazi fantasy and the Poles of the Marxist version were likewise utterly remote from the real world: mere sentimental abstractions.

10. W Shakespeare, *Henry IV, part two*, act IV, scene 5.

11. A Finkielkraut, *The undoing of thought*, London: Claridge, 1988.

12. D O'Keeffe, 'Diligence abandoned: the dismissal of traditional values in the school', in D Anderson (ed), *The loss of virtue*, London: Social Affairs Unit/ New York: National Review, 1992, pp 183-199.

13. Note, for example, the 'sensitising sessions' now so common in higher education, especially in the United States.

14. The subject has not been fully analysed but we think that there is a marked overlap between the ideological preoccupations and outlooks of some personnel in these services.

15. For recent comment on the British case, see E G West, 'Education without the state' in A Seldon (ed) *Replacing welfare after the lost century*, London: Institute of Economic Affairs, 1996, pp 11-19.

16. See the brilliant treatment by S Yates, *Civil wrongs: what went wrong with affirmative action*, San Francisco: CS Press, 1994.

17. A Flew, 'Self-improvement and its neglect by the contemporary mainstream churches', in Anderson, op cit, pp 211-227.

18. Yates, op cit.

19. Scruton, op cit.

20. R Lynn, *Educational achievement in Japan: lessons for the west*, London: Macmillan Press, 1988.

21. D O'Keeffe, *The wayward elite*, London: Adam Smith Institute, 1990.

22. A Seldon, *The riddle of the voucher: an inquiry into the obstacles of introducing choice and competition in state schools*, London: Institute of Economic Affairs, 1986.

23. W Glasser MD, *Schools without failure*, New York: Harper and Row, 1969.

24. *The New York Times*, 29 January, 1992, pp A8-A9.

25. Ibid.

26. Ibid.

27. Much the same spirit of argument and unstable compromise happens in the case of British education.

28. A Flew, 'Competition and co-operation: equality and elites', *Journal of Philosophy of Education*, Vol 17, no 2, 1983, pp 23-54.

29. T R Sizer, *Horace's compromise: the dilemma of the American high school*, Boston, Houghton:Mifflin, 1992.

30. B S Cooper, *Magnet schools*, London: Education Unit, Institute of Economic Affairs, 1988.

31. J Nathan, *Public schools by choice. Expanding opportunities for parents, students and teachers*, Minneapolis MN: Institute for Learning and Teaching, 1989.

32. B S Cooper, 'The politics of privatisation: policy-making and private schools in USA and Great Britain' in W L Boyd and J G Cibulka (eds), *Private schools and public policy*, London: Falmer Press, 1989, pp 254-268.

33. A S Bryk, V E Lee and P B Holland, *Catholic schools and the common good*, Cambridge MA: Harvard University Press, 1993; J S Coleman, S Kilgore and T Hoffer, *High school achievement*, New York: Basic Books, 1982; J S Coleman and T Hoffer, *Public and private schools. The impact of communities*, New York: Basic Books, 1987; J Chubb and T M Moe, *Politics, markets and America's schools*, Washington DC: The Brookings Institution, 1990.

Chapter 5

1. Economist William Nordhaus of Yale University estimates, in *Managing the global commons* (Boston: MIT Press, 1994) emissions stabilisation at 1990 levels would generate a net discounted cost of $7 trillion.

2. J Shanahan 'The Environment', in *Issues '96: the candidate's briefing book*, Washington DC: The Heritage Foundation, 1996, p 110.

3. Remarks made on April 2, 1993 by Perry Pendley, president of the Mountain States Legal Foundation in Denver, Colorado, which is representing the ranchers in this case.

4. 'Bird-Watching at the EPA', *The Washington Times* editorial page, July 28, 1993.

5. R Crandall, 'Why is the cost of environmental regulation so high?', Center for the Study of American Business, Policy Study Number 110, February 1992.

6. J Porritt, 'Seeing green: how we can create a more satisfying society', *One Earth*, Findhorn Foundation, The Park, Forres, Scotland, Winter 1988.

7. Personal interview with Dr S Fred Singer, Science and Environmental Policy Project, Fairfax, VA, January 8, 1997.

8. M Bookchin, 'We can't heal the environment without remaking our society', *The Progressive*, Madison, WI, August 1989.

9. *Monthly Review*, New York, NY, June 1989.

10. Porritt, op cit.

11. Sierra Club fundraising letter to members, December 20, 1996, San Francisco, CA.

12. D L Ray, *Trashing the Planet*, Washington DC: Regnery Gateway, 1990, p 16-18.

13. J Hoyt, 'The Rights of Animals', *Earth Ethics*, Spring/Summer 1996, p 22.

14. From the transcript of the proceedings at the Sixth Annual Western Public Interest Law Conference, March 5, 1988, University of Oregon Law School.

15. G Easterbrook, 'The Birds', *The New Republic*, March 28, 1994, p 27.

16. D Murdock, 'Putting lizards first', *The Orange County Register*, November 21, 1993.

Chapter 7

1. D H Lawrence, 'John Galsworthy', repr *Selected Essays*, Penguin, 1954, p 224.
2. 14 August, 1996.
3. Cf F R Leavis's classic essay 'Reality and Sincerity' reprinted in *The Living Principle*, 1975, in which he contrasts one ordinarily sentimental poem with one by Emily Brontë and, as an example of achieved sincerity-and-reality, Hardy's 'After a Journey'.
4. I Murdoch, *The Sea, The Sea*, 1978, p 67.
5. Ibid, pp 79-80.
6. Ibid, p 80.
7. Hilda D Spear, *Iris Murdoch*, 1995.
8. Alice Walker, *The Color Purple*, The Women's Press, repr 1991. *The Color Purple* is an epistolary novel in which one series of letters is written by the heroine Celie in the dialect that Mark Twain gave to Jim in *Huckleberry Finn*, and the parallel series by her nearly educated sister Nettie mainly in Africa.
9. Ibid, p 82.
10. Ibid, p 164.
11. Ibid p 167.
12. Cf Ian Robinson and David Sims, 'Ted Hughes's *Crow*', *The Human World* no 8, 1972.
13. M Amis, *London Fields*, p 114.
14. Ibid, p 98.
15. Eg ibid, pp 91, 149, reports of darts and football.
16. I am not alone in this judgement. Cf S W Dawson's essay on Iris Murdoch in *The Pelican Guide to English Literature*, and the review of *The Information* in *Private Eye*.

Chapter 12

1. E Gellner, 'James Frazer and anthropology' in R Mason (ed) *Cambridge Minds*, Cambridge: Cambridge University Press, 1994, p 211.
2. J Z Muller, *Adam Smith in his time and ours*, New York: The Free Press, 1993, p 49.
3. De Rougemont, *Love in the Western World*, Princeton: Princeton University Press, 1983.
4. H A Guerber, *The Myths of Greece and Rome*, London: George C Harrop & Co, 1907
5. M Drabble (ed), *Oxford Companion to English Literature*, Oxford: Oxford University Press, 1989, p 1085.
6. M Drabble, *The Witch of Exmoor*, London: Penguin (Viking), 1996.